CHOOSING
Cheer

CHOOSING
Cheer

Experiencing the Joy of Jesus in
the Everyday and Unimaginable

Nicolet Bell

Morehouse Publishing
19 East 34th Street
New York, NY 10016

Morehouse Publishing is an imprint of Church Publishing Incorporated.

Library of Congress Cataloging-in-Publication Data has been applied for.

ISBN 978-1-64065-796-0 (hardcover)
ISBN 978-1-64065-797-7 (ebook)

To Josie Lou, my miracle.

Your life has brought me immeasurable joy.
I pray that the joy of Jesus would be
your strength all the days of your life.

Contents

Introduction

The forecast was less than promising.

The outdoor ceremony was scheduled for Saturday at 5 p.m., the same time the weathermen were calling for severe weather and potential tornadoes. As the wedding drew closer, the forecast became increasingly dire.

Severe storms likely to produce tornadoes were to begin at 5 p.m. "It's fine!" my future sister-in-law said as her plans for a gorgeous ceremony under the most beautiful live oak trees evaporated.

SATURDAY, 1 P.M.

I glanced up at the sky to see the sun peeking around white, fluffy clouds with blue skies scattered between them. We couldn't believe it! It was a beautiful day. But would it last? The forecast still looked grim. "At least we are getting to take beautiful pictures outside," I commented.

SATURDAY, 4 P.M.

As the sun peeked through the clouds, the weather seemed to be holding off. Guests were beginning to arrive for the ceremony as we all huddled out of sight in the cottage.

"I think we're going to make it!" the wedding planner said. And with that, we all relaxed. After a whole day of waiting and holding our breath, we were almost at the finish line.

The violin began to play, and as I held the hand of my daughter—the cutest flower girl you've ever seen!—and the arm of my husband—the most handsome man I've ever seen!—we made our way down the aisle without a drop of rain. As I stood in my spot up front and watched our beautiful bride make her way to my baby brother, I thought, "You just never know about the weather!

SATURDAY, 7 P.M.

The bottom fell out of the sky. It rained buckets and buckets as the wind ripped through the beautiful, strong oak trees. Fortunately, we were all safe and dry inside the reception venue. The lightning popped, and thunder shook the building, but you could barely hear it above the band's trumpets. There were no power outages, no tornadoes, just a beautiful evening celebrating the newlyweds.

CLOUDY WITH A CHANCE OF TROUBLE

The weather predictions change by the hour in South Mississippi, where I live. Just like the weather predictions were off for the wedding ceremony, on any given day, if you look at your weather app when you roll out of bed in the morning, the forecast is almost sure to change by your midmorning snack. It may be forty degrees in the morning, eighty degrees in the afternoon, and back down to thirty degrees in the evenings. The weather in Mississippi reminds me of one of my favorite passages where Jesus says to his disciples:

> These things I have spoken to you, that in Me you may have peace. In the world you will have tribulation; but be of good cheer, I have overcome the world. (John 16:33, NKJV).

Other translations exchange the word "tribulation" for "trouble" and that helps us to understand what Jesus is talking about (NIV). He doesn't say, "It's cloudy with a chance of trouble," or "There's a slight chance of trouble in the forecast." Did you catch it? Jesus says that we WILL have trouble. Unlike the weather reports in South Mississippi that change by the hour, this prediction is unfortunately assured. It's a promise. We like to think of the promises of God as only good things. It's hard for us to look at this and think "Yes! Trouble is a promise of God."

Fortunately for us, there are multiple promises in this verse. Yes, Jesus promises that we will face trouble in this world. That is our reality this side of heaven. Since the fall of creation, things have not been as God intended. But at the same time, in the same breath, the same sentence, He is also promising that He is with us, that we can have peace and joy in Him, and that He ultimately has overcome the world.

We like peace and joy, and we want to avoid trouble. Like the forecast on my brother's wedding day, John 16:33 feels less than promising. It's actually very promising, but do we like the warning/promise combo it makes?

Sure, peace and joy in any circumstance sounds nice, but do we see this truth in our lives when the storm clouds well up and the rain starts to pour down? If I'm honest, I am usually still surprised when trouble shows up in my life. I know Jesus tells me it's coming, but I am still taken back, left in surprise or shock when life throws me something I don't expect. Often, amid hurt, the last emotion I feel is cheerfulness or joy. You, on the other hand, may find yourself in the opposite place. Maybe your life has been full of disappointment and hardships with no end in sight. Maybe you have been stuck in a pattern of sadness for so long that you would be shocked or surprised if something good came your way.

That's the beautiful thing about the words of Jesus. They meet us wherever we find ourselves. If we are sad or happy, angry or excited, Jesus commands us, "Be of good cheer; I have overcome the world." Whether it's a diagnosis, a marriage, a test grade, or a parent-child relationship, we've all been in a place where we are hoping for the best outcome despite the prediction. When the diagnosis is hopeless, we've prayed for hope. When the relationship seems over, we keep trying. Though Jesus promises that we will face trouble on earth, He also promises that we will experience the fullness of his joy. This sounds great, but how?

WHY CHOOSING CHEER?

From the time I could walk, I think I had a pair of pom-poms in my hand. I was born in the middle of a family of cheerleaders, and very early on, I cultivated a love for the sport. Since I was a little girl, my mother instilled in me that cheerleading wasn't just an activity we participated in; cheerfulness was a lifestyle. It was an outlook that we had on life. Especially as believers in Jesus, we could always find a reason to be cheerful.

In middle school, I discovered the verse John 16:33. Choosing Cheer is my life motto. It's about choosing the joy of Jesus even in challenging circumstances. As a little girl with a bow in my hair and a spring in my step, I had no idea how this attitude would impact my life.

As I grew older, I began to understand that this mindset was not only a biblical concept but, more convincingly, a command from Jesus himself. It reminded me that cheerfulness had nothing to do with a uniform but everything to do with a state of the heart.

I've long since retired my pom-poms, and doing a backflip is out of the question, but the truth of this verse remains with me. And what's true for me is also true for you. When you still feel empty even though you are surrounded by beautiful things. When you're surrounded by heartbreak, loss, and confusion, and you find yourself thinking, "There's got to be more than this." God's promise of joy is still true for you.

If someone was to ask you "Do you want more joy?" I don't think your answer would be, "Nah, I'm good." We all have a desire for joy deep within us, placed there by God and designed for Him alone to fill.

Cheerfulness used to be as easy as breathing for me. Unfortunately, as I've aged, I've had more and more experiences with heartbreak and loss, hurt and confusion. Now, it seems that remaining joyful is more of a challenge.

How do we remain cheerful amid difficult things? That's what this book is all about. We'll unpack and wrestle with how to truly experience this cheer—this joy—that Jesus says we have access to as his followers. I don't know about you, but I want more cheer in my life. I want to experience the fullness of life that Jesus has for me.

Will you join me on this journey?

PART ONE

Why Choosing Cheer?

ONE

Choices

E very day, we make choices. From the moment we wake up, we are faced with decisions. What will I wear today? What will I have for breakfast? Should I exercise? Who will I sit by? Who will I talk to? Will I put that load of laundry in now or later? What should I make for dinner? Should I have that conversation today or tomorrow?

A lot of these choices seem small as we make them, but at the end of the day, the culmination of our choices results in how we have spent our time.

Each day, we have a choice. We can choose to focus on Jesus (who he is and how he is with us) OR we can choose to focus on the chaos around us. So often, we allow our circumstances to control our feelings, emotions, and reactions, but the ultimate truth that we find in scripture is that the choice is ours.

From the beginning, Adam and Eve had a choice—to eat of the fruit or to trust in God. Joshua tells the people following God after the exodus, "Choose this day whom you will serve. . . . as

for me and my house, we will serve the Lord" (Josh. 24:15). Jesus
himself teaches, "do not worry," and he instructs us to "consider"
or "think on" certain things to decrease our anxiety and to remind
us of what is important (Matt. 6). The letters of Paul highlight
the concept of our choices; he writes, "think about these things"
(Phil. 4:8) and "take captive every thought to make it obedient
to Christ" (2 Cor. 10:5, NIV). In other words, by the help of the
Holy Spirit, you have some say over what you are thinking. From
the beginning to end of the scriptures, we are reminded that we
have choices and that our choices matter.

To understand the concept of Choosing Cheer, we must understand that we have been given choices by God. In our focus
verse, John 16:33 (NKJV), Jesus says we will have trouble, "but
be of good cheer, I have overcome the world." Other translations
say, "but take heart." It's as if Jesus is saying, "You can expect
trouble in this life, but you have a choice of how you are going
to respond to it." This doesn't mean we ignore hard things or
sugarcoat tragedy, but what it does mean is that we know and
cling to the One who has the power to help us experience true
joy and peace amid anything that comes our way.

A CHOICE

I was alone in my house, laying on the couch, tears leaking out
of my eyes, palms spread across my abdomen, mourning the life
that had been and now wasn't, knowing that I would never hold
those precious fingers, never wash those precious toes, or feel that

heartbeat next to mine while rocking my baby to sleep. It was a pain I didn't know existed. A sadness I didn't think was possible.

A few months before this, I had taken the step of faith to launch Choosing Cheer—at the time, a blog—where I began to explore this concept the Lord had been teaching me for years with others through writing. I remember laying there and reciting John 16:33, wrestling with Jesus and asking Him "where is the cheer in this?" All I felt was pain—both physical (from the surgery) and emotional. In this deep struggle with God and His word, He began to teach me what this concept really meant. It had been a nice and tidy concept until trouble showed up in a gut-wrenchingly painful way. Jesus says in this passage, you are GOING to have trouble. It is a promise, but we're often surprised when trouble comes.

That was the case for me as I lay there on the couch. Everything I thought about my future, the way I'd imagined the next six months or sixteen years, had changed—in an instant. The years that stretched out before me full of bottles and scattered toys evaporated in a moment's time. All I could see was a cloud of sadness stretching over my coming days.

But it was also a moment when God became real to me. I felt His presence so close to me even as the tears fell onto my cheeks. I was assured that He was real, and He was with me even then. Even though my heart was hurting and I couldn't see the future, I was certain He had not abandoned me and He had good plans for me. The Lord helped me to begin to untangle my joy from my circumstance and revealed several lessons.

The problem we face is that our joy is often tied to our circumstances. Some circumstances we have control over, and others are out of our control. Those that are out of our control are the hardest for us to come to terms with. Whether that is losing a job, gaining a responsibility, suffering an illness, losing a loved one, or getting a diagnosis, we don't like interruptions with how we thought our lives were going to go. It can leave us confused, hurt, disappointed, frustrated, and even outright angry at God. How do we make sense of where we find ourselves?

OTHER BOATS

One of my favorite stories about Jesus recorded in the Gospels comes to mind as an example to help us understand how to respond when trouble comes our way. This passage describes Jesus and His disciples after a very long day of teaching. The crowds were so great that Jesus got into a boat to teach so everyone could hear Him. He taught all day, speaking in parables.

When evening came, Jesus told His disciples "Let's go to the other side." Jesus was tired, worn down, and weary from the demands of the people. We know this because the scripture describes that He goes to the back of the boat and goes to sleep. Mark depicts a storm that wells up with overwhelming wind and waves, causing the boat to rock violently. The disciples go to where Jesus is to wake Him. Panicking, they ask Him, "Teacher, do you not care that we are perishing?" He wakes up and speaks out to the storm, "Peace! Be Still!" Then the rain and wind stopped, and there was "a great calm" (Mark 4:35–41).

Most of us first learned this story about Jesus calming the storm in Sunday school or our children's Bibles, or maybe Vacation Bible School. Then, we probably heard sermons on it or encountered it in Bible study as we grew up. The thing about familiar stories is that we often skip over or miss important details. Think about an infamous story in your family—you know, the one your grandfather tells *every* year at your Christmas gathering. My husband's family are big fishermen, so fishing stories color my memories of Christmas gatherings at the Bell's home on the Mississippi Gulf. As we all know, fish stories grow each time they are told. As our family recounted these tales, the fish seemed to get bigger at each family gathering. When listening to the stories, if it was a familiar one, sometimes my mind would wander and tune out. It can be the same way with familiar Bible stories we learned in Sunday school—it's easy to overlook the details in a story we're familiar with.

As I was reading this story a few years back, I noticed a sentence I'd never noticed before: "And other boats were with him" (Mark 4:36). This statement is not recorded in Matthew or Luke; only Mark includes this detail. This may seem like an insignificant detail to most people, but the day I read this passage, it had significant meaning. This brief sentence reminded me that the storm I was going through was not in vain. The winds were picking up and the waves were tossing me about, threatening to throw me over, but the people in the other boats were watching. Would I run below in panic like the disciples, hysterically flailing my arms, sure that this would be the end? Or would I be like Jesus—asleep and sure of God and his sovereignty over my situation?

The Message translation says it like this, "Other boats came along." This is an interesting thought. Others came along in the storm. They were witnesses not only to the storm but to the power of Jesus at work in the storm. They witnessed Jesus speak out, "Peace! Be still!" and saw the wind and waves respond to His voice. They witnessed the "great calm" that Mark describes. If the other boats wouldn't have been there, the miracle would've been done in secret and the glory of God would not have been on display.

It's the same in our lives. God does not cause the storm, but He is in control of the storm. While we are on this side of heaven, we will face trouble. It is a promise. We shouldn't be surprised or panicked when it shows up. We shouldn't run in distress, asking God, "Do you even see us? Do you even care?" God doesn't cause the storm, but He can use the storms in our lives to show the other boats watching that He is God. He is in control. He wants others to witness His peace, His calm, His joy in our lives even in unimaginable circumstances.

Sometimes He stops the storm, sometimes He just rides in the boat with you for a while, but either way He will get the glory. Other people will see your calm in the midst of the storm, and they will want to know more about Jesus. Jesus tells us over and over again that we will be the way people see and experience

Him in the world. We will be His witnesses. That's how other people will come to know Him.

Our problem is that our joy is most often tied to our circumstances, but Jesus wants to set us free from that roller coaster of ups and downs and give us lasting joy found only in Him. The day I read this passage in a new way, God met me on my couch, in my pain, and He reminded me that He knew exactly what it felt like to lose a child. That when He willingly gave up his son Jesus for my sake, He knew the pain that I felt in that moment. I realized that when Jesus spoke these words that are recorded in John 16:33, He didn't just say them haphazardly. Jesus said them as one who understood trouble, understood struggle, and understood pain but "for the joy that was set before him endured the cross" (Heb. 12:2).

This gives us a picture of what joy in Jesus looks like. I don't imagine Jesus had a smile on His face when He journeyed up that hill to his crucifixion, but I do know He had joy. Because joy is a part of his character and his very nature, it wouldn't have been stripped from Him at that moment. It would have been refined, actualized, and realized in that time of intense trial. He gives meaning to the words James penned:

> Count it pure joy, my brothers and sisters, whenever you face trials of many kinds, because you know that the testing of your faith produces perseverance" (James 1:2–3, NIV).

Jesus's work on the cross is the ultimate example of this scripture lived out. Again and again, He was deemed innocent by

Pilate, but He kept his mouth shut, a sheep led to the slaughter. He knew why He came and stayed focused on that purpose. Despite the suffering He endured, His joy remained constant.

FULL CIRCLE

At the time we lost our first baby, I was serving as a youth pastor in a local church. Our loss happened on a Wednesday, and we were forced with a choice. As I was going back to surgery, our lead pastor asked me, "What do you want me to tell the kids?" I thought about it for a minute, and then I said, "The truth."

I didn't know how to describe it at the time, but I felt a distinct leading from the Spirit to be honest about what we were dealing with. As pastors or church leaders, I don't believe that we should parade our problems for sympathy or attention, but I also don't think we need to pretend like we have it all together. Authenticity is one of the biggest encouragers of genuine faith.

After our loss, one of the first people I called was my youth pastor's wife from when I was growing up because she had been open about her pregnancy loss. I knew it was important for me to do the same. At the time, I didn't understand the significance of this decision, but as the weeks passed, I started receiving cards, text messages, and phone calls from parents of our students describing the conversations they had with their families. Sitting around the dinner table answering questions like,

- "Why do bad things happen to good people?"
- "Why did God take Nicolet's baby?"
- "If Preston and Nicolet are following Jesus, why did this bad thing happen?"

Our transparency allowed discipleship to happen in others' homes. Our openness allowed for transformative conversations in families. For years, my prayer for this group was for God to work in their homes. I knew I only had influence for a few hours a week, but their parents had the most influence on their faith. This may seem like a strange answer to that prayer, but our youth group kids and their parents were the other boats in our storm. They watched, paid attention to what was happening, and asked crucial questions.

While this didn't take the pain away, I look back now and know that it helped me to make sense of some of the pain. God was taking our mess and our hurt and working for good to draw people to himself. We saw Genesis 50:20 lived out: "You meant evil against me, but God meant it for good."

One of my favorite commentaries, *The New Daily Study Bible* by William Barclay puts it beautifully:

> If we believe that in Jesus we see the picture of God, then, in the face of amazing love, it becomes not easy but at least possible to accept even what we cannot understand, and in the storms of life to retain a faith that is serene. (Barclay 2017, 178)

When I am going through something, I often stop and look around to see what other boats are present. Our faithfulness certainly isn't dependent on the approval of others, but we're called to be witnesses to the love of God in all circumstances. My hope is that we would learn how the joy of Jesus, refined in our trials, makes a difference in our everyday lives and in the lives of those in the other boats beside us.

Cheer Practice

Let's take a moment to put into practice what we have learned. If there is anything I learned in my time cheering, it is the importance of practice. We didn't just magically hit our routines and tumbling passes. It took months (often years) to nail all our skills. When I was cheering in college, there was a stint where we had 6 a.m. practices and 6 p.m.–10 p.m. practices daily, with class in between. Some mornings, it was so hard to get my body to cooperate and flip backward on the gym floor at 6 a.m.

Looking back now, I know those moments are the ones that formed me and made me not have to think twice when throwing the same skill in a high-pressure moment at a game. It is often the quiet, unremarkable moments that prepare us for the big moments. Our faithfulness and discipline in the small things shape us for the big things. Paul writes in 1 Timothy 4:8, "While bodily training is of some value, godliness is of value in every way, as it holds promise for the present life and also for the life to come."

Just as practice was necessary every day when I was cheering, it is essential for experiencing this "good cheer" Jesus is referring to in John 16:33. For our purposes together, we will call this Cheer Practice. We'll hold this practice together at the end of every chapter and rehearse a few things that will help us live a cheerful life.

For those of you who aren't familiar with the cheer or dance world, the callout or signal to begin a routine or a tumbling or stunting skill is always "5-6-7-8." This is part of what is called an eight-count, which is the cornerstone for coordinating a group to do any type of choreography. Each number in an eight-count is assigned to a certain movement that makes up the skill or dance. For example, before doing a back handspring, the callout would be "5-6-7-8," "5-6" would be a clap, "7-8" arms by your side. Then starting "1-2" sit back and bend your knees and jump, "3-4" arms hit the ground to support while flipping backward in a handstand motion, then "5-6" legs pop down, for a final "7-8" where legs straighten, and arms return to the side. Whatever skill or dance routine, "5-6-7-8" is always the beginning. We'll use this call out, the start of an eight-count, to help us in our spiritual disciplines throughout the book.

5—*Breath Prayers*

Breath prayers are short meditations to help you focus on the giver of breath. Breath comes from God and breath connects us with God. The breath prayers I will share at the end of each chapter are invitations to remember that God is God and we are not. That He is in control and our job is to be still in trust.

The practice of breath prayer has many benefits. Breath prayers have helped me experience more of the joy of Jesus—despite my circumstances. In my own life, when anxiety ramps up, and my mind is running in circles, I stop and say a breath prayer. It centers me, calms me, and focuses me. We know that breathing by itself has many statistical benefits in calming our minds. Combining breathing with focus on God through scripture increases the benefits.

This is not a new prayer concept, but it is, perhaps, a forgotten one. Christians have been practicing contemplative breath prayers for centuries. It began in the monasteries and made its way out into the daily spiritual disciplines for many years. Perhaps in our rat race and rushed pace of life, we have become too busy to appreciate the significance of these ancient practices.

I was first introduced to the power of intentional breathing when I tried yoga for exercise after I injured my back in my last year of cheering. I had a herniated disc with nerve pain running down my left leg. I went from being a college athlete, strong and in shape, to dragging my leg along, unable to run or do any of the skills I was used to doing daily. That landed me on a yoga mat. I had tried yoga in the past, but never a restorative class. In some restorative classes, you never get up off the mat, moving slowly from one relaxing pose to another, holding them for long periods of time, often with the support of props, and an emphasis on controlled breathing.

The poses and stretching we did were so great for my injured back and leg, but I completely underestimated the benefit of learning controlled breathing. As I slowed down my breathing, I would feel closer to Jesus. I didn't understand why at the time, but later I was introduced to breath prayer and these experiences began to make sense to me. Breathing can help us experience His peace and love. In my own life, breathing has helped me to experience more of Jesus's joy and cheer, and I believe it can do the same for you.

Breath prayer is pretty simple. Choose a short phrase that is rooted in scripture and pray it on an inhale and exhale. Let me give some examples:

Keeping with the eight-count theme, the pattern of a breath prayer could look like this:

- Inhale: one, two, three, four
- Exhale: five, six, seven, eight

Try breathing and meditating on the words or saying the words aloud on those counts:

- Inhale: In His Presence
- Exhale: is the fullness of joy

Another example from our key verse:

- Inhale: Jesus has overcome
- Exhale: Be of good cheer

Sometimes I repeat the phrase one time and then just breathe the counts. Other times, I repeat the phrase over and over again. There isn't a perfect way or formula. The goal is to slow down our minds and bodies and connect to God through his word. As we practice together, breath prayers will be a tool you can use to reduce anxiety and increase trust and cheer.

6—Scripture Callout

In cheer practice, we would memorize callouts that would serve to help the team know which cheer we were about to perform. Memorizing scripture (or Scripture Callouts) is one of our greatest tools as followers of Jesus. In our fast-paced society, it is often underutilized.

Tips for memorizing scripture:

- Write the verse or passage on a sticky note and put it on your mirror or dash.
- Take a screenshot and put it on the background of your computer or phone.

- Break down the verse. Try to learn or focus on one phrase at a time.
- Say the verse out loud.

For our first callout, let's work on memorizing our theme verse for the book:

> In the world you will have tribulation; but be of good cheer, I have overcome the world. (John 16:33, NKJV)

Practice saying this verse out loud.

7—Gratitude Challenge

I believe that gratitude is the best prescription for cheerfulness. When we think about the things we have to be grateful for, it is hard to stay focused on our challenging circumstances. In Philippians 4, Paul prescribes gratitude:

> Do not be anxious about anything, but in everything by prayer and supplication with thanksgiving let your requests be made known to God. And the peace of God, which surpasses all understanding, will guard your hearts and minds in Christ Jesus. (vv. 6–7)

Paul emphasizes the role of thanksgiving in reducing anxiety and promoting peace. We know that peace and joy go hand in hand. Where there is peace, joy will follow.

Thankfulness is not always something that comes natural to us. We have to practice.

I encourage you to write down three things that you are grateful for today.

Thank you, Jesus, for:

_____

_____

_____

8—Spread Some Cheer

A simple way to choose cheer in our lives is to share cheer with others. We often overlook these simple ways to connect with others and share the love of Jesus. I pray that during our study together, we will intentionally spread cheer, or joy, with those around us.

TODAY'S CHEER CHALLENGE:
SHARE A SMILE!

Sharing a smile is one of the simplest ways we can spread cheer. Intentionally looking up from our phones or our grocery lists to look someone in the eyes and smile at them can make a big impact on their day.

One of my coworkers and mentors, Dr. Ronnie Kent, has a saying that I love. He often says, "Practice makes progress, Jesus makes perfect." I love his spin on the old saying "practice makes perfect." I heard this saying in the cheerleading and dance world so many times as we went through a routine for the 400th time! In Philippians 4, Paul writes, "What you have learned and received and heard and seen in me—practice these things, and the God of peace will be with you."

In our study together, we are after progress. Jesus is the only one who has perfection. If these Cheer Practice sections at the end of each chapter move us toward a closer relationship with Jesus, we will be making progress. We'll leave the perfection up to Jesus.

TWO

Promises

W hen I was in middle school, my whole family went on a ski trip with our church youth group. My brother, four years younger than me, was allowed to tag along, because my parents served as chaperones.

My dad grew up in the Northeast and was a great skier. The rest of us grew up in South Mississippi, where there isn't much opportunity to practice our snow skiing skills. It was my and my little brother's first time skiing, and needless to say, he picked it up way quicker than me—he's always been more athletic. I was pizza-ing/snow plowing my way down the easiest slope on the mountain, my dad sticking close by me, when my little brother came whizzing by us. We came to a curve about that time, and I didn't turn enough. I went right off the path, past the orange tape, and into a grove of trees. I had enough sense to fall before hitting a tree, but I took a tumble, and my ski pole ended up in my back. My dad rushed over to me, along with some of my older friends in the youth group who were more experienced skiers.

We didn't realize my brother was missing in the chaos of checking on me.

We looked around and called for him, then quickly realized my ten-year-old brother was lost. Nowhere to be seen. My dad left me with my friends and took off to find him.

We figured he was at the bottom lift or the next slope over. As the sun set, we all gathered for dinner at the cabin, yet there was still no sign of my brother or dad. This was before cell service was accessible in the mountains, and my mom panicked. Finally, hours later, they emerged. They were freezing and worn out, but relief was all over my dad's face.

While we waited, uncertain of what was happening, my dad was looking for my brother. He'd called in the ski patrol to help, and he wasn't going to stop looking until he found my brother. When we asked my brother later if he was afraid while he was lost, he said, "Not really. I knew Dad would find me." He had confidence that he wouldn't be alone for long.

Jesus wants us to have that same childlike confidence in him. I didn't have to ask my dad why he spent all day and evening looking for my brother. I knew the answer—my brother is his. He belongs to him, he's his responsibility, his love. There's no way he would've stopped looking for him. Jesus was able to be of good cheer in the face of trouble, because He knew who He was, and He knew his relationship with his father. Jesus desires for us to have that same confidence. It is possible for us to Choose Cheer if we are confident and sure of who we are and our relationship to Jesus.

Leading up to his statement to be of good cheer in John 16:33, Jesus shares what scholars call the "farewell discourse" between Jesus and his disciples. Think of it like a halftime speech during the Super Bowl. They are His final words to His disciples before the big event—His death and resurrection. The farewell discourse begins with the Passover dinner. He washes the disciples' feet, a filthy task reserved for servants. Then, He gathers them around the dinner table and begins to teach them. Some key points emerge in this conversation that are essential to understanding how to choose cheer amidst challenging circumstances.

YOU ARE HIS

An overarching theme throughout the farewell discourse (John 13–17) is identity. Jesus invites His disciples to come with Him to his Father's house. He tells them that He will prepare a place for them in a little while. "In my Father's house are many rooms," Jesus promises his disciples (John 14:2). He wanted the disciples to know that in heaven, there is room for all who will come. Jesus assures his friends that though they will encounter rejection on earth, they won't be rejected in the Father's house. On earth, doors may be shut by their families, friends, and strangers, but the Father's door is wide open to them. Knowing we have a forever home, a place we belong, helps us to feel a sense of belonging while we are still on earth.

My dad didn't search for my brother out of obligation but out of love. He was his, and he pursued him at all costs. It's the same with God—Jesus is the ultimate example of God's pursuit of us as his children. In sending Jesus to earth in the form of a human, God displayed his ultimate love for us. Jesus came to make a way for us to be with God. After Jesus tells His disciples He is preparing a place in the Father's house for them, they ask, "How can we know the way?" And Jesus responds, "I am the way" (John 14:5–6). God sent Jesus in pursuit of us and sent Him to show us the way back to Him. We belong to God, we are His children, and He has made a way for us to go home to Him.

Continuing, Jesus tells the disciples, "I am in the Father, and you in me, and I in you" (John 14:20). Through this statement, He reveals the communion and connection He is offering to those who follow him. Jesus then promises His love to them, "He who loves me will be loved by my Father, and I will love him and manifest myself to him" (John 14:21). He knows that circumstances are about to get tough for his disciples and that they will need to have an identity rooted in who He is and their relationship to Him to withstand the challenges that are coming. As Paul writes later in his first letter to the church in Corinth, "You are not your own, for you were bought with a price" (1 Cor. 6:19–-20). Jesus knew what was about to take place, the encouragement his followers would need, and what encouragement you and I need today. We are his. May we rest in that truth today.

YOU ARE NOT ALONE

Jesus continues His final discourse by giving His disciples a promise to hold on to. He tells them, "I will not leave you as orphans, I will come to you" (John 14:18). As he talks about leaving, He continues to explain how He will come to them. Jesus tells them He will send them a helper and goes on to explain this Helper, the Holy Spirit, and what his role will be (John 14:16; 26). He assures them again to "not let their hearts be troubled," and "neither let them be afraid," for "I will come to you" (John 14:27–28). He knew the disciples would need to remember this truth in the trials they were about to face. They were not alone. He wants you to remember the same truth. You are not alone.

A 2023 report from the US Surgeon General names a public health crisis, an "Epidemic of Loneliness and Isolation" (Office of the Surgeon General (OSG) 2023). The study found that almost half of the adults in the United States report experiencing loneliness. This number was the highest among young adults. The report noted that "lacking social connection can increase the risk of premature death as much as smoking up to 15 cigarettes a day." Today, we are the most connected that we've ever been through technology and constant communication, but we are also the loneliest we have ever been.

Knowing that Jesus is with us gives us power. Knowing that we aren't alone gives us strength to face things we don't think we can face. Jesus knew this truth firsthand, and over and over again, He reminds himself that the Father is *with* Him. Jesus is telling

His disciples that even though His physical presence would be going away soon, He was sending his spiritual presence, the Holy Spirit, to be with them. Jesus knew His Father was with Him and it gave Him strength to face the cross. When we know that our Triune God—Father, Son, and Spirit—is with us, we are given the strength to face anything we might encounter on the way.

YOU ARE WORTH IT

As Jesus continues in His farewell discourse, His final lessons to His disciples before His death, He gives them another promise. Jesus says, "Greater love has no one than this, that someone lay down his life for his friends" (John 15:13). We read this as people who know the rest of the story, but let's take a minute and think about what this would have sounded like to the disciples upon hearing it. They wouldn't have known what He was talking about. Laying down his life? The disciples surely would have felt confused. This verse gives us two promises from Jesus:

1. You are a friend of God.
2. You are worth dying for.

Jesus gives his disciples two other truths to hold on to. They are His friends, and they are worth His sacrifice. When thinking about what He was about to endure on the cross, Jesus tells the disciples that even though they are going to leave Him, "I am not alone, for the Father is with me" (John 16:32). Jesus was confident in His relationship to the Father. In the same way, we are to be confident in our relationship with Him. Because of this truth, Jesus persevered to the cross despite the abandonment of his friends. He knew they would desert Him, and He loved them anyway.

He desires us, wants us to spend time with Him, and wants us to know Him intimately like we know our best friends, even in our imperfection. Our relationship with Him is more significant than any earthly friendship we can imagine, even the best ones. In his perfection, He took on our imperfection to rescue us. He didn't question our value or our worth when He was going to the cross; we shouldn't question it either. Jesus tells us, "You are my friend, and you are worth it to me."

Like my dad who diligently searched all over the mountain for my brother, pushing through his exhaustion and fear, Jesus went to the greatest lengths to prove His love to us. We can be confident in our relationship with Him because it has been sealed by His blood on the cross and his resurrection from the grave. We didn't earn it; we don't deserve it; it is a true gift of God. This confidence gives us the strength to face our everyday lives as well as life's heartaches and hiccups.

You can have joy

CHRISTMAS MORNING, 1999

All year I had been waiting. All of my friends at school already had one, but I had to wait until Christmas. Living on a schoolteacher and small business owner salaries, special items were reserved for special occasions. I had my eyes on an American Girl doll. Her name was Josephina. I had flipped through the catalog until the pages were falling out and had carefully selected this doll. She looked like me with her slick black hair, dark eyes, and tanned skin. She was the one I wanted. I remember rounding the corner on Christmas morning that year to find her standing on the couch, my Christmas dream come true! I jumped up and down and hugged my parents, "She's here! She's here!"

What's your favorite gift you've ever received? Take a moment to picture it, remember it. Who gave it to you? For what occasion? How did you feel when you received it? In His final discourse, Jesus talks about a gift He is giving us and He says it will be the best one we've ever received. In this passage, Jesus gives one more promise, one more gift to His disciples. He tells them, "You can experience my joy." He describes it multiple times as "the fullness of joy."

When we see something repeated in the scriptures, we should pay special attention to it. The authors of the Bible didn't have font formats to bold, italicize, or highlight. When something was important, they repeated it. What does Jesus mean when He says the fullness of joy? Perhaps He knew and understood we would struggle with only experiencing part of it, or occasional joy. Jesus makes it clear here that His desire for us is more than that. Jesus wants to give us a spectacular gift—*all* of His joy. Will we unwrap it?

FULLNESS OF JOY

My dog, Mr. Trek, loves to sit in the sunshine. He will follow a sliver of sunshine coming through our big window as it moves about the room throughout the day. He will laze in one spot until the sun moves to another spot, then he moves over there. Constantly chasing the warmth, the glow. There's a point in each day that as the sun rises it no longer hits that specific window and that makes for a sad puppy dog. There's a period when it is directly overhead and no rays come in through the windows. Then, the sun sets enough that it comes through the back window, and I can usually find Mr. Trek, having migrated to a new spot to enjoy the afternoon rays.

I think so often this is what our experience with joy looks like. We bask in slivers or rays of joy, and then it moves just enough to be out of reach and unattainable. So, we chase it. Maybe because of our situation, maybe for no apparent reason at all, but it seems like we only glimpse it before it rises to the other side of the house. We move around, trying to find it, having a little luck here or there, but nothing that lasts.

We weren't made to chase rays. We weren't designed to seek little slivers of sunshine. They leave us craving more, looking around for more light. Jesus's desire is for us to walk out the door and step into the full sunshine, letting the full light of the sun coat every inch of our skin, warming us to our very bones, and he wants us to stay there. Jesus tells His disciples as He continues his farewell discourse, "These things I have spoken to you, that my joy may be in you, and that your joy may be full" (John 15:11).

If Jesus wants us to experience the fullness of joy, complete joy, why does it so often seem far away like something we read about and see other people experience, but don't really experience ourselves? I think too often we undervalue the Holy Spirit's role as Joy-giver. Jesus promised us a Helper, the Holy Spirit. He promised us that we don't have to do it alone. In fact, we can't. Jesus talks about joy and peace being the gifts of God that we can experience *through* the Holy Spirit.

When describing his death, He tells the disciples, "You will be sorrowful, but your sorrow will turn into joy" (John 16:20). The example Jesus uses here is childbirth (John 16:21–22). I think He's speaking to us, ladies. He certainly wasn't speaking from His personal experience on earth. Childbirth is painful, messy, and just plain hard, but once that precious baby is placed in your arms, joy replaces the pain. It doesn't take away the pain, but the joy outweighs the pain.

Jesus says it will be like this for His disciples concerning His death and the persecution they will face after His death and resurrection. This echoes promises from the Old Testament where God "give them beauty for ashes" (Isa. 61:3, NKJV), and He will "turn for me my mourning into dancing" (Ps. 30:11). This is not a new concept in scripture, but Jesus is giving it new meaning and direct application into the disciples' lives, and our lives today.

Jesus ends His farewell discourse with a strong statement saying, "These things I have spoken to you, that in Me you may have peace. In the world you will have tribulation; but *be of good cheer*, I have overcome the world" (John 16:33, NKJV).

I have studied and meditated on this passage for years, and I believe Jesus is offering us the key to experience his peace and his joy. This whole book—this whole concept of Choosing Cheer—is built around this verse. There's a simple truth here, a greater promise that anchors our understanding. To *Choose Cheer*, you must believe Jesus has overcome the world. When Jesus spoke these words, His crucifixion and resurrection hadn't happened yet, but He was so sure of His victory over death that He could say them in confidence. We can read His words with the same assurance. Do we believe that Jesus holds the victory over hell and death? Do we believe that nothing is stronger than Him or too hard for Him?

If we genuinely believe that He has overcome the world, Jesus's promise to His disciples, "no one will take your joy from you" (John 16:22) is also our promise. Your circumstances may change, your physical possessions may be taken away, your status may be lost, but no one can take your joy away. If no one can take our joy away, why do we so often *not* experience it?

Sometimes, we give it away. Sometimes intentionally, most of the time unintentionally.

 Cheer Practice

Reunion

My alma mater recently invited me back to a football game for a cheerleader alum weekend. They had a cheer camp for children of alums and invited us to perform with the current squad in the pregame routine. Excited to kick the dust off my old moves, I made plans to attend the weekend. There was only one problem: I was not in as good shape as when I was cheering in college. They held a practice the night before, and I remembered most of the moves, thanks to muscle memory, but I quickly realized I jiggled in places I didn't ten years before.

The current squad taught us the changes they had made to the fight song routine. The fight song is perhaps the single most crucial piece of choreography for a cheer squad. It is the routine you perform the most. Therefore, it becomes ingrained in your memory. At sixty, my mother still remembers every move to her college fight song and can perform it perfectly. The issue with this alum performance was that my body remembered the old way of doing the fight song. The motions we had performed hundreds, maybe thousands of times, were so stuck in my head and muscles that learning the simple changes was almost impossible.

As we took the field on the big night, I heard the familiar sounds of excitement right before kick-off—the sounds are different from the turf than in the stands. There is a more incredible excitement, almost electrifying. As my hands wrapped around the pom-poms, it took me years back. As the band took the field and the pregame routine began, I fell right back into the motions and routines. However, when we performed the fight song, I messed it up in four places. Despite my rehearsing, the old muscle memory prevailed. I would have needed another week to perform the routine multiple times daily to learn the new motions seamlessly.

We also have muscle memory when it comes to our spiritual disciplines. The more reps we put into praying, worshiping, and reading scripture, the more ingrained the motions become in our heads and hearts. The more we practice them, the easier they are to incorporate into our everyday lives.

It works the other way as well. It can be hard to create those habits when we aren't practicing spiritual disciplines. That's what these Cheer Practice sections are for. Spending some time cultivating these habits will help them become ingrained in your muscle memory.

5—Breath Prayers

Pray this scripture on an inhale and exhale.

- Inhale: one, two, three, four
- Exhale: five, six, seven, eight

Try breathing and meditating on the words or saying the words aloud on those counts.

- Inhale: I am not alone
- Exhale: for the Father is with me
  (John 16:32)

- Inhale: No one will take
- Exhale: your joy from me
  (John 16:22)

Remember, there isn't a perfect way or formula. The goal is to slow down our minds and bodies and connect to God through his word. Sometimes I repeat the phrase one time and then just breathe the counts. Other times, I repeat the phrase over and over again. Any combination is good, as long as you are focusing on Jesus.

6—Scripture Callout

Memorizing scripture is such an important part of practicing the presence of God.

Our second callout:

You make known to me the path of life; in your presence is the fullness of joy. (Psalm 16:11)

Practice saying this verse out loud, repeat it, write it down, and put it somewhere that you can see it.

7—Gratitude Challenge

I believe that gratitude is the best prescription for cheerfulness. When we think about the things we are grateful for, it is hard to stay focused on our challenging circumstances. Thankfulness is not always something that comes natural to us. We have to practice.

I encourage you to write down three things that you are grateful for today. This could be in relation to what we've studied in this chapter or just related to something in your life right now. I encourage you to think of something different from the last chapter.

Thank you, Jesus, for:

_____

_____

_____

8—Spread Some Cheer

A simple way to choose cheer in our lives is to share cheer with others. We often overlook these simple ways to connect with others and share the love of Jesus. My prayer is that during our study together, we will be intentional about spreading cheer, or joy, with those around us.

TODAY'S CHEER CHALLENGE:
REMIND SOMEONE OF THEIR WORTH!

In this chapter, we studied how God calls us friends and how we are valuable to Him. When we know this about ourselves, it's easier for us to share that same worth and value with those around us. You could buy a coworker a coffee on your way to work or write a friend a note and stick it in the mail. It doesn't have to be complicated. Letting someone know that they are seen is an easy way to remind them they are valuable. How can we show someone in our life that they are loved and valued by God today?

PART TWO

What Cheats Us
from Cheerfulness?

THREE

Challenges

U nderstanding what something is helps us define what it's *not*. For example, ice cream is cold and creamy, not warm and soupy. Tea is sweet and iced, not unsweet and hot (some of you may disagree, but I'm a Southern girl at heart). As I began to study what cheerfulness is, it was just as helpful to study what it's not. Cheerfulness is a state of the heart, not a fleeting or passing feeling. However, it is often regarded that way in our lives. What it is not could also be described as what prevents cheerfulness from flourishing in our lives.

Certain mindsets and behaviors can prevent us from embracing cheerfulness. Both scripture and my personal experiences offer numerous examples of this, so I began to write down what I discovered. As I reflected on my list, I identified common themes that could be categorized into four groups. To aid in remembering them, I came up with a catchy alliteration. Let's refer to these as the Four C's That Cheat Us of Cheerfulness: Challenges, Confused Connections, Comparison, and Control.

The first C that robs us of cheerfulness is Challenges. Choosing Cheer does not mean that we ignore the hardship or suffering around us. It's not a Pollyanna way of approaching life. We want to be present and aware of our suffering and the suffering of those around us, just as Jesus was attentive to the needs and sufferings of the people around Him. So, how do you choose cheer while also being honest about the reality you are in?

James addressed this as He opens His letter:

"Count it all joy, my brothers, when you face trials of various kinds, for you know that the testing of your faith produces perseverance. And let perseverance finish its work, so that you may be mature and complete, not lacking anything" (James 1:2–4).

Here in James, we are instructed to count it all as joy when we face trials of many kinds. This is not an easy task. It can seem wrong to walk around cheerful while there is so much pain and suffering. Parts of the world are at war. People around me are hurting, I saw a homeless man on the street corner earlier today. People I love have terminal cancer, and the list goes on and on. With so much hurt around us, isn't it insensitive to be joyful?

At the height of the COVID-19 pandemic, my team was working on a social media post for our church and we were looking at an image and I said, "We can't use this picture—he just looks too happy." As I reflect on that statement, I think that's often our problem—we confuse happiness with joy/cheer.

Let's think about Jesus. As we noted in the previous chapter, when Jesus went to the cross, He suffered great pain. I don't believe He was smiling, and I doubt He was happy. But I believe

He was filled with joy. It's a part of His character, and a fruit of the Spirit. Joy doesn't disappear when times get tough. Jesus had joy amid great suffering because He had hope. He told the robber next to Him who asked for forgiveness, "Today you will be with me in paradise" (Luke 23:43). Jesus was sure of His hope. He knew where He was going, and that allowed Him to have joy, even in the most brutal circumstances.

The Greek word for "cheer" that Jesus uses in this passage is "chario" and it means more than a holiday cocktail or a chant to say at a football game. It has the same root as the Greek word for joy, "chara," which is used throughout scripture. It is defined as "full of cheer, calmly happy or well-off, be well, be glad, to rejoice joyfully" (Baker 2013, p. 2322). Joy and cheer are so similar in meaning that they can be used interchangeably.

"Calmly happy" as described in this definition sounds a little bit like peace to me. In verse 33, right before Jesus says, "Be of good cheer," he says, "I have said these things to you, that in me you may have peace." We can conclude from this that peace, cheer, and joy go hand in hand. This definition also says that being cheerful means being "well." Who wouldn't like to be well? Wellness is a hot topic in our culture right now and we pursue it in various ways. From diet fads, to supplements, to medications, to the latest and greatest exercise routines, to acupuncture, to retreats, we chase after wellness. Jesus says that cheerfulness and joy are crucial to becoming truly well, but we often don't chase joy the same way we chase whatever is trending in society.

Over the course of this book, we will unpack how to uncover this cheer, joy, and peace that Jesus describes. Jesus says it is ours to grab onto, but we often don't feel or experience it in our lives. Sometimes we're tempted to think that if we follow Jesus, our lives will be easy. *But our reality is that cheerfulness is a challenge.*

REFLECTION FROM AN (ALMOST) SHARK ATTACK

Throughout most of my summers growing up, I visited the Alabama Gulf Coast or Florida Panhandle, as they are conveniently located a short drive over from Mississippi. These trips are characterized by sunshine and laughter every year, with hours spent in the water and strolling along the shore.

Occasionally, there would be a weird manifestation of jellyfish or seaweed overtaking the Gulf, but for the most part, the trips were uneventful and the biggest thing we were worried about was our feet burning on the scalding sand. But on a recent trip, things got especially weird.

A few days before a large group of my family went down to the beach, we read about a shark attack in the popular 30A area of Florida. A young woman lost her arm and leg in pretty shallow water. This is very rare for our part of the Gulf. Sharks are usually not a threat unless you go out to the deep waters.

In the days following the attack at 30A, more sharks were spotted, lots of them. Videos from drones were circulating on the internet showing them swimming in very shallow water, right next to swimmers. However, this was further down the beach than us, so we weren't too concerned. On our first day on the beach, we noticed something very unusual. "Look at those fish! In the waves!" my brother-in-law yelled out. As my eyes found the fish, my jaw hung open. It was unlike anything I had ever seen before. As far as the eye could see, a massive school of fish was swimming in both directions. When a wave would crest, we could see a wall of fish. Of course, we weren't afraid of the fish, but we were a little skeptical about what might come after the fish, so we kept looking out into the water, more cautious than normal.

Several of us returned to the rental house a little early to wash off and prepare for dinner, but my parents stayed behind for some extra beach time. "There was a big one!" my mom exclaimed when they got back that evening. "At least six feet! Right by the shore!" I looked at my dad to see if my mom was being dramatic or truthful. When he nodded his head, I knew she was serious.

In the summer on the Alabama Gulf, it is so hot at the beach that you have to get in the water frequently to cool off. We got in a practice of getting out of the water when the school of fish would move in close. We would return to the water once the current pushed the fish further away from the shore. Several of us were in the shallow water watching a school of fish a little further out. Suddenly, my aunt shouted, "There he is!" She came up out of her beach chair so unusually fast, we all jumped up with her. My eyes followed her pointing finger straight to a shark moving very quickly toward my cousin's son about knee deep in the water.

It only took one glance at my cousin, who was on the shore holding her one-year-old, to realize that she didn't see what we were seeing—her six-year-old knee deep in the water with a shark swimming straight toward him. I took off running and snatched Jax out of the water by his arm. I then continued down the beach in the direction the shark was swimming to a group of little girls whose mother was up further on the shore. I haven't felt an adrenaline rush like that in years, maybe ever. When the coast was clear (literally), we all took some deep breaths. I said a quiet, "Thank you, Jesus," that no one was hurt.

This shark was a smaller one—probably four feet, maybe five feet—but it was FAST. I have never seen a creature move that fast in the water. I always pictured seeing a shark like you see in the movies—an ominous fin peeking out on top of the water. This shark was on the bottom of the ocean floor, with no fin in sight. Thankfully, the water was clear, which allowed us to see it.

Later, under the group of umbrellas, my husband joked, "Babe, I haven't seen you run like that in two years!" As we were giggling, Stella, Jax's older sister who was seven years old, overheard and chimed in, "I wish there weren't any sharks." Preston and I glanced at each other, registering how this event must have alarmed her. "Sharks aren't always bad," I replied. "They are an important part of the ecosystem, and they usually stay away from us."

She thought about that, and said, "Could be. But I still wish there weren't sharks." We nodded as she continued, "I really wish there was nothing dangerous or sad in the whole world. Why does there have to be sad things?" I was processing this question, readying my reply when she kept going, "Like my birth mom and dad."

My eyes grew big, and my heart grew sad. I was reminded how much she had experienced in her short little life. Triggered by the fear of the shark, she was reminded that all is not well in the world—that there are dangers that make us afraid.

When Stella and Jax came to live with my cousin and her husband through the foster care system, they were dropped off with only the clothes on their back. Stella was covered in sticky maple syrup, and Jax was running a 103 fever. At less than two years old, Stella had learned to climb onto the counter to reach a cup and the sink to get herself and her baby brother some water. She had figured out how to survive and care for herself and her brother in extremely challenging circumstances. When she first came to live with my cousin, she wouldn't eat hot food. If her food was hot or warm, she wouldn't touch it. She had only had cold food her whole little life. Jax was born early at thirty-four weeks old addicted to meth. His traumatic birth brought with it a host of health and behavioral problems.

Over time, they began to adjust to life with a loving family who adored them. Visitations and drug testing proved that reunification with their birth parents would not be an option. After 694 days, Stella and Jax's adoption became official. I thank God that He was watching out for them, and that trouble hasn't had the final say in their lives.

Stella moved past the incident and continued to play with my daughter, Josie, in the sand. As I watched her, I thought about what she has seen and experienced that my daughter will most likely never experience. The verse that seeped its way into my thoughts at that moment was John 16:33 (NIV), "In the world you will have trouble."

I looked at her adoptive mother and whispered to the Lord, "She has seen trouble, but she has also seen grace." The second part of that scripture also came to mind, "but be of good cheer, I have overcome the world." Stella's life testifies to just how evil the world is, but more than that, her life testifies to just how good God is.

I thought about how I would answer Stella's question, if I could go back to that moment: "Why does there have to be sad things?" I think you and I could agree that there is no easy answer to this question. In scripture, Jesus gives us assurance that trouble will not have the final word. Sad things will happen while we are on this side of heaven, but they will not be the end.

It is easy for us to let our challenges or troubles control the outcome of cheer or joy in our lives, but Jesus reminds us that regardless of our circumstances, even really terrible ones, we don't have to live in fear. We can experience and enjoy freedom in Jesus and joy in His presence. We can have cheer and spread cheer when it comes from a place of promise.

HEART WARRIOR

When I think about challenges, I think about my friend Kristen.

If you follow Highway 42 in Petal past the high school I attended, the elementary school I attended, the church I grew up in, on out into the next small town, and then into the next little community, over two bridges and then a sharp left turn, you'll wind up on an old red dirt road with craters the size of beach balls. As you turn left, the first house on the left belonged to the Henderson family. If you keep bumping down the road, your car will get coated in that thick red dirt, and you'll come to the second house on the left, an old farmhouse that belonged to the James family. Pastures and a pond separated these two properties.

Growing up as the baby of six brothers and sisters, my mother would tell stories of a life outside on the James farm. The stories would range from digging potatoes, picking peas, playing basketball, or tussling with her siblings. Oftentimes, the stories would include the Henderson family, the farm right up the road. One particular story I remember is how a nickname came to be. Frequently, the siblings would host kickball, dodgeball, or baseball games, and often, the ball would wind up in the Henderson's pasture.

"Lee! Ball!!" someone would call. Lee, the younger next-door neighbor, would retrieve the ball and join in on the game, earning him the nickname, "Lee ball." Lee would eventually marry and have a daughter who would become one of my best friends.

Kristen and I share a friendship that runs a generation before us, as old as that red dirt road. We didn't go to school together, but we were thick as thieves. We began with playing Barbies and as we grew up, we surely perfected our karaoke version of The Wreckers—hitting our different harmony parts perfectly, hairbrushes in hand.

Kristen was my most steady friend. When other girls weren't always nice or kind, I knew I had a true friend that loved me for who I was. She was the matron of honor in my wedding. Though we didn't go to the same college or run in the same circles, and though I moved away right after I got married, we've managed to stay in touch over the years.

We may not talk every week, but when we do talk, we pick up right where we left off the time before. One day, I picked up the phone and heard my friend on the line, "Nicol, something isn't right with his anatomy scan. We have to come up to Jackson for more testing." Kristen was pregnant with her third baby and received some unexpected news.

Jackson, Mississippi, houses the only pediatric hospital in the state. After coming up for their appointment, we learned that Colson had been diagnosed with Tetralogy of Fallot with Pulmonary Atresia and a large VSD—in regular terms, a very complex congenital heart condition. He would require life-saving medication and a heart cath to place a temporary stent as soon as he was born. A few months after, he would undergo his first open heart surgery to correct the anatomy in his heart.

Colson was born on October 12. From the very beginning, he had a light—a joy that was contagious. His big, round baby blue eyes and wide, sweet smile made him look perfectly healthy. However, doctors had cautioned my friend that his heart required urgent assistance. A heart catheterization was performed, providing a temporary solution to ensure oxygen flow to his body.

On February 28, Colson underwent his first open heart surgery at just four months old. Following a twelve-hour surgery, the surgeon delivered disappointing news. He hadn't been able to accomplish what he had hoped, and they would need to leave his chest open in case further surgery was required. In the early hours of the morning following his surgery, around 2 a.m., Colson's heart stopped beating. Thanks to the vigilant medical team, they promptly responded to the emergency and resuscitated him.

Kristen wrote this reflection on her Facebook page several months after this experience:

"My soul continually remembers and is bowed down within me. But this I call to mind, and therefore I have hope: the steadfast love of the Lord never ceases; His mercies never come to an end; they are new every morning; great is your faithfulness" (Lam. 3:20–23).

Ten weeks ago, I sat in a PICU room, watching a doctor do compressions on my four-month-old's open chest after a ten-hour open heart surgery. The only word I can use to describe how I felt in those long minutes is helpless. I couldn't do anything to make it stop or make it better. I couldn't do anything to save my baby. I sat in silence, as tears flowed down my face, saying over and over, "Please, God." That's all I could do, quietly beg Him to intervene.

Colson has had so many prayers prayed for him, before he was even born. For a while, I truly believed God would heal him and he wouldn't need surgeries at all. **Even though that** didn't happen, the Lord has always let me know He's right here. Every time I've had a scary thought or doubt, no matter how small, He whispers reassurance in my ear. I even thought one time in the hospital, "What if he's cold? He can't wake up or cry to let me know he's cold." God answered immediately, "He's fine, I've got him." He has not been silent—not while I was pregnant, not when Colson was born, and not during his surgery and sickness. He stayed close and made sure I felt Him and heard Him when I needed reassuring. We haven't had to walk this journey alone, and I know we won't ever have to. He is right here with us.

There is not a day that goes by that I don't see Colson for the miracle and gift he is. The baby we didn't plan for (because we thought our family was complete) completely turned our world upside down, in the BEST way! For a long time, I wondered why. Why does he have to have a complex heart condition? Why does he have to be put through so much? Why do his siblings have to witness their baby brother be sick? WHY HIM?

But now I know. I KNOW that God chose Colson and wants to use him for good and for His glory. I don't believe He gave our baby a heart condition. But I do believe He knew what our baby would face, allowed it, and said, "He is MINE." God turned something so difficult and terrifying into a beautiful testimony for His glory. Isn't that all we can ever hope for? To be used for the glory of the Almighty? What a perspective change for this mama! I am thankful, and will forever be thankful, for our special little boy that we never thought we'd have. And I'm even more thankful that I know Jesus, and I never have to walk alone.

Ten days after she wrote this, they returned to Jackson for a routine check-up. They were finishing up their rounds, thinking they had a good report and were about to head home, when Kristen noticed something was off with Colson. As she studied him, she realized he was quickly deteriorating, and she knew he was really sick. She rushed him to the nearest medical team member. They quickly found out he had an aneurysm in his heart. The staff immediately gave him medicine to stabilize him and made plans for another open-heart surgery to remove the aneurysm. They would do the surgery first thing in the morning. We waited. We prayed.

It was hard to believe this sweet baby had experienced another complication, but it was also hard to ignore the hand of God in his little life. My friend lives three hours away from the pediatric hospital. This could have been a different story if they had been at home when this happened. The fact that they were at the children's hospital when this happened could have saved his life.

The following morning, May 16, Colson underwent his second open heart surgery at just seven months old. After the surgery was complete, he had a significant amount of bleeding that they tried to get under control. The surgeon said there was nothing else he could do at that point. The bleeding was so intense that a team of nine doctors and nurses worked for five hours straight trying to stop the bleeding and giving him blood transfusions. Kristen describes this moment as feeling completely helpless. She uttered prayers on behalf of her baby boy and watched the medical team work.

They were finally able to get the bleeding under control, but Colson ended up on ECMO, a machine that pumps blood through his heart mechanically. We prayed and we waited, begging God to allow his heart to beat on its own again.

It was Sunday morning, May 19, three days after the surgery—the morning the doctors planned to attempt to wean Colson from the ECMO machine. A baby could only stay on this machine for five days, so his coming off the machine was imperative. The gravity of the situation was so great, the magnitude of the next several hours pressed in close.

All of the family's friends and acquaintances asked people to pray for Colson. Word traveled across the Southeast, and across the country, to pray for Colson this Sunday morning. As a result, people were lifting up his name to God in church services nationwide. The procedure was scheduled to start at 8 a.m. but was delayed a few hours. It's no coincidence that most church services were held at the exact time of his procedure. People were praying everywhere.

While Colson was in the OR, my sweet friend Kristen and her husband tuned in online to the service at our home church where our former pastor was leading the church in praying for Colson. Brian prayed for God to wake up Colson's heart and allow it to beat on its own again. In the middle of the church service, my friend received a call from the OR. Colson was off ECMO, and his heart was beating! Her family members sent a message, and it was announced during the service.

Then the most powerful thing happened: As my friend watched the online service, she witnessed the church's response. Everyone was on their feet, cheering and celebrating, clapping and shouting thanksgiving to God for answering their prayer! Their rejoicing bled into worship. God had done a miracle, and they were the collective witness.

Colson still had such a long way to go. He was not healed, but his heart was beating. And that was enough for that moment. That was enough to remind all of us who witnessed that God still answers and responds to the prayers of His people. We believed a miracle had occurred, and the response was pure, unabashed joy as we cheered and applauded the God who hears and answers prayers.

As I write this chapter, Kristen is still in the hospital with her baby boy. They've been in the hospital for almost four months this time, and Colson still has such a long way to go. Their story isn't wrapped up in a pretty bow, and it may not be for many years. So we wait and we pray.

God has already used Colson's story as a mighty testimony, and I believe He will continue to. As Kristen wrote in her Facebook post, I don't believe God caused his heart defect, but I do believe that He is using this family's story to reveal His power and glory, His intimacy and His care, even in the most helpless circumstances.

Kristen has been the epitome of *Choosing Cheer* in this season. She has remained steady and positive even during great hardship. When I would visit her in the hospital, we almost always ended up laughing: her joy, her light, not dimmed by the chaos around her. Sure, she has hard days and moments when she feels like throwing in the towel—moments when she misses her big kids so much it is a physical ache, but Kristen has the assurance of Jesus. That's the only way I can describe it. His presence, his joy, is buoying her up against the wind and waves. As she wrote, "Even though it didn't happen . . . I know Jesus and I never have to walk alone."

"Count it all joy . . . when you meet trials of various kinds" (James 1:2) can be a hard command to swallow. James writes that these trials produce perseverance that finishes its work so that you may be "mature and complete, lacking in nothing." My friend has a new understanding of this verse. Jesus says that as His followers, we will share in His glory, but He says to do that, we must also share in his suffering. On this side of heaven, we can't have one without the other.

Whatever storm you find yourself in, the same Jesus that has sustained my precious friend wants to sustain you. Maybe you find that you have a pulse but that your heart feels dead. Maybe the prayer we prayed for Colson's physical heart is a prayer you need to pray for your spiritual heart. Maybe you need to ask God to wake you up. To allow your heart to beat again.

# Cheer Practice

5—Breath Prayers

Pray this scripture on an inhale and exhale.

- Inhale: one, two, three, four
- Exhale: five, six, seven, eight

Try breathing and meditating on the words or saying the words aloud on those counts.

- Inhale: Blessed is she
- Exhale: who remains steadfast under trials
  (James 1:12)

- Inhale: Nothing can separate me
- Exhale: from the love of God
  (Rom. 8:38)

6—Scripture Callout

Memorizing scripture is such an important part of practicing the presence of God.

Our third callout:

Count it all joy . . . when you meet trials of various kinds.
(James 1:2)

Practice saying this verse out loud, repeat it, write it
down, and put it somewhere that you can see it.

7—Gratitude Challenge

I believe that gratitude is the best prescription for cheerfulness. When we think about the things we are grateful
for, it is hard to stay focused on our challenging circumstances. Thankfulness is not always something that comes
natural to us. We have to practice.

I encourage you to write down three things that you are
grateful for today. This could be in relation to what we've
studied in this chapter or just related to something in your
life right now. I encourage you to think of something different from the last chapter.

Thank you, Jesus, for:

_____

_____

_____

8—Spread Some Cheer

A simple way to choose cheer in our lives is to share cheer
with others.

TODAY'S CHEER CHALLENGE:
SUPPORT SOMEONE IN A CHALLENGING TIME.

In this chapter, we discussed challenges and difficult circumstances. Ask God to show you one person that is having a challenging time right now and a way you can support them. It could be a card in the mail, a meal, or a hug. It doesn't have to be complicated. When I was going through an ongoing health crisis, I experienced an outpouring of love and support. People showed up at my house to help me take care of Josie, a baby at the time, or they brought food. I had one friend that would just come and sit with me. Cards from family and friends who weren't local filled my mailbox. All these seemingly simple acts of kindness helped carry me during that challenging time. The love of friends and family sustained my joy even in the difficult circumstances. How can you show that type of love to someone today? Is there someone in your life who needs an encouraging text or card? Perhaps a meal or a food delivery gift card?

Small acts of kindness can remind people that they are seen and loved in the midst of challenging times.

FOUR

Confused Connections

*E*very little girl needs a pair of pom-poms.

My daughter loves to visit my mom's house. Nana always surprises her with something, like a pack of stickers or a coloring book, whatever she might have picked up at the dollar store. On one of our recent visits, my mom handed Josie Lou a pair of red and silver sparkly pom-poms, saying, "Every little girl needs a pair of pom-poms." Even though they were cheaper than the ones they give out at stadiums, Josie's eyes widened as she waved her new pom-poms, jumping up and down, exclaiming, "Hooray, hooray!" Almost immediately, Josie Lou turned to me, held one of her pom-poms out to me, and said, "Mommy, this one's for you!" As I took the pom-pom out of her little hand, she said, "You do hooray, Mommy!" So we walked around the house waving our pom-poms and shouting, "Hooray!"

As I reflect back on this sweet memory, I'm reminded of a couple of things. First, we have an innate desire to share our cheer. Josie Lou was so excited about her pom-poms, she immediately wanted to share them with me. She desired me to share in her joy. It wasn't enough for her to experience it on her own. She wanted me to experience it *with* her.

Second, cheer is contagious. When we witness someone experiencing genuine and unadulterated joy, we instinctively want it. Just as Josie Lou wanted me to experience joy over her new pom-poms, I also desired to share her joy. When I saw the bright smile on her face, I couldn't stop a grin from spreading across mine. When we love people, we want to share in their joy.

We can experience the true joy of Jesus in our relationships with others. In His second letter to Timothy, Paul writes, "I long to see you, that I may be filled with joy" (2 Tim. 1:4). Jesus taught us the significance of our relationships with many of His parables and lessons focusing on how we relate to others. While our relationships bring us immense joy, they also have the potential to deprive us of joy. This highlights the Second C that can cheat us from cheerfulness: *Confused Connections.*

REDEEMING RELATIONSHIPS

Jesus valued relationships. His earthly ministry and the lessons He taught are evidence of this fact. Jesus could have carried out His ministry alone. Instead, He invited others into His close circle to become His disciples and learn from Him.

Jesus's miracle at a wedding in Cana also sheds light on the value Jesus places on relationships. Jesus's very presence at the wedding emphasizes the importance and value of marriage as a worthy reason to celebrate. When the host family ran out of wine—a cause for embarrassment to the family—Jesus heeded His mother's request to help by turning water into wine, sparing them public humiliation.

A beautiful aspect of this miracle in John 2 is that it wasn't put on display for the guests of honor. All they knew was that they had good wine; the best was saved for last. It was the servants—the lowest of the low—who fully witnessed this miracle. This teaches us how Jesus values the least and the last, the forgotten and the lost, not just the wealthy and influential.

From the very beginning, Jesus demonstrated with His actions what kind of connections were important to Him. This is evident in His selection of followers. Following this miracle, He continued to expand His group of disciples. He gathered a motley crew, or as someone from the South might say, "Fellas who had no business running together." Among them were fishermen, a tax collector, a zealot, and a winemaker—individuals who were total opposites in their ideas and beliefs. The group Jesus gathered made no sense to those looking in from the outside or to those on the inside, for that matter! Each choice Jesus made was intentional, demonstrating that, in his presence, even the most unexpected connections can be used for a greater purpose.

HISTORY OF RELATIONSHIPS

Throughout the narrative of scripture, the biblical authors highlight the value of relationships. Beginning in Genesis 1, we see that connections and relationships are essential to life with Yahweh. God exists in a relationship understood as the Trinity—God the Father, Son, and Holy Spirit. Because we are made in the very image of God, we also long for connection. After God created Adam, He said, "It is not good that the man should be alone," and created Eve. After humanity rebelled against God, God chose to redeem all of creation through a family.

When Jesus walked the earth, His entire ministry was one of relationships and connection. When He ascended to heaven, He sent us a helper, the Holy Spirit, to be in relationship with us and help us in our relationships with others. At the end of time, we will celebrate at a marriage supper of the Lamb. We will be gathered together as one family, one connection. From the beginning to the end of the story of scripture, relationships are in every line.

It is clear in the scripture that relationships and connections are intended by God to be good things. It is also clear in the scriptures that we mess this up. From Adam and Eve with the first temptation and the fall, to Jesus's interactions with the Pharisees, the story of scripture reminds us that our connections can be challenging and even costly.

Some of my most precious memories are with the people I am most connected to. At the same time, relationships are the source of some of my biggest regrets and deepest heartaches. I imagine the same is true for you. When we are connected deeply to those around us, we open ourselves up to deep hurt. At our very being, we are wired for connection, but when we place our human relationships before our relationship with God, we can end up disappointed and dissatisfied. We can often experience confusion in our connections when we seek them as our primary source of joy.

The good news is that Jesus is in the business of redeeming and restoring our relationships. He is actively working in us and around us to restore our relationships to the way that He designed them to be enjoyed. When we seek Jesus first, we can find true joy in our connections.

UNLIKELY CONNECTION

One of my favorite accounts from the Gospels is Jesus's interaction with the Samaritan woman at the well. You may already be familiar with this passage, but I invite you to explore it with me with fresh eyes. Jesus was traveling with the disciples through the region of Samaria. This fact alone should be enough to stop us in our tracks. Any good Jewish man would travel *around* Samaria, no matter how out of the way it was. The Jews hated the Samaritans and believed that they were unclean. They didn't speak or interact with Samaritans for fear of becoming unclean themselves. However, in typical Jesus fashion, He guided his unlikely crew of disciples along an unexpected path straight through Samaria.

It was the heat of the day when they came upon a well. Weary from the journey, Jesus sat down while He sent His disciples ahead to find food. Shortly after, a Samaritan woman approached the well to draw water. It's worth noting that it would be very unusual for a woman to be at the well in the heat of the day. Typically, women would come to the well in the morning or at night due to the intense midday temperatures. They would also go in groups to gather water. The timing of this woman's trip to the well and the fact that she was alone reveals something about her. She was a loner. By coming to the well when nobody else was around, she avoided being seen or having to engage with others. (If you've ever run to the grocery store, crossing your fingers that you won't bump into anyone, you may be able to relate.)

When she approached the well and saw a Jewish man, I'm sure she was surprised, and I imagine she assumed he wouldn't speak to her. As she prepared to draw her water, Jesus turned and addressed her, "Give me a drink" (John 4:7). She replies, "How is it that you, a Jew, ask for a drink from me, a woman of Samaria?" The woman couldn't believe Jesus was speaking to her, let alone asking for a drink of water. Jesus replied, "If you knew the gift of God, and who it is that is saying to you, 'Give me a drink,' you would have asked him, and he would have given you living water" (John 4:9–10).

Puzzled, the woman asked, "Where do you get that living water?" She didn't understand what He was talking about, but she was curious and wanted to know more. I envision Jesus gesturing toward the well as He explained, "Everyone who drinks of this water will be thirsty again," and then turning back to the woman and adding, "but whoever drinks the water that I will give him will never be thirsty again. The water that I will give him will become in him a spring of water, welling up to eternal life." Without hesitation, she looked at Jesus and said, "Sir, give me this water" (John 4:11–15). She didn't have all the answers; it didn't all make sense to her, but something about Jesus and something about her desperation generated her faith.

Jesus continues in the conversation, pursuing the woman's heart and addressing the root of her sadness and shame. "Go, call your husband, and come here," He requested. She replied, "I have no husband." I picture her lowering her gaze in that moment, only to lift her eyes in surprise as Jesus replied, "You are right in saying, 'I have no husband'; for you have had five husbands, and the one you now have is not your husband. What you have said is true" (John 4:16–18). Jesus understood that the woman's pain and shame were rooted in her past relationships. Although we may not know all the details, it's clear that her history with relationships was troubled. Yet, Jesus saw directly into the heart of the matter. His knowledge of her past didn't deter Him from engaging in dialogue with her or offering the life-giving water that leads to eternal life.

Friend, maybe this is something you need to be reminded of today. No matter what your past looks like, no matter what mistakes or troubles you've faced, Jesus knows and wants to address it with you. Not to inflict punishment or shame, but to offer you the living water that wells up to eternal life. No matter your background, your social status, your marital status, your sins, your victim status, your choices, your failed relationships, your hurt, your shame, your guilt, the same living water He offered the unlikely woman at the well, He offers to you.

Maybe you've felt like you have been counted out of God's story. Maybe you feel like He's forgotten you or abandoned you. Maybe you feel He doesn't see or know what you are going through. Maybe this is why your joy is absent or fleeting, only coming occasionally in short bursts. Hear this truth today— Jesus sees you. Jesus loves you. Jesus offers you living water that wells up to eternal life. Just as Jesus broke through all barriers to connect to the Samaritan woman, today He breaks through all barriers to connect with *you*. Your relationship with others can only be as strong as your relationship with Him.

The woman's connection with Jesus gave her such great joy that she immediately wanted to share with others, even people she had previously avoided. Like Josie Lou wanted to share her precious pom-poms with me, the joy we receive from Jesus should compel us to connect with others. When we approach relationships from a place of fulfillment in Jesus, we are much more likely to experience joy in our connections. If we approach relationships from an empty place, looking to human relationships as the source of our joy, we'll be left disappointed and frustrated. This applies to any relationship—marriages, family members, friendships, or coworkers.

The Samaritan woman at the well was the first person to whom Jesus revealed His true identity. He explained that He was the Messiah, the promised one who would save the world. Their conversation underscores just how much Jesus cares about our relationships. His connection to this woman sheds light on what Jesus values, how He interacts with us, and how we are to interact with others.

AWKWARD BEGINNINGS

Walking across campus to my communications class every Tuesday and Thursday, I kept noticing a guy named Preston, whom I'd met before but didn't know too well. We had a few mutual friends, and because we were both athletes—I was a cheerleader, and Preston ran track—we occasionally saw each other in the athletic facility.

One day, while we were walking in the same direction, he spoke to me. He said, "Hey, I'm Preston. I think we both are friends with Alex." I agreed and we talked about how we had seen each other in the athletic center. Walking to class together soon became our routine. On our walks (I was secretly swooning), we would fall into step with each other and chat about our days.

Shortly after we started walking together, our conversation went in a new direction. As we were walking, Preston looked at me, then looked down, and said "So, my fraternity is having this date party next week. I'm not sure if I'm going to go or not because I have a test the next day, but if I do decide to go, would you go with me?" It was the most awkward date invitation I'd ever received. Who asks someone out just in case they decide to attend an event? But I gave him my number and told him to let me know what he decides.

The week passed without any communication from Preston. No messages, no calls. As the date party approached, I accepted the idea of not attending. On the afternoon of the event, I received a text from a new number, saying, "Hey, I think I'll go tonight." I felt somewhat annoyed at this point and didn't even want to go anymore. Perhaps I wanted to prove a point to him for leaving me hanging. But, with no other plans and intrigued by his deep blue eyes and genuine smile, I texted back, "Great! I'll see you there."

If you're expecting a tale of a wonderfully romantic evening, you'll be disappointed. It turned out to be an awkward night. I couldn't figure out if Preston had invited me to be nice or if he actually liked me. We had some good conversation, but mostly, it was limited by the loud music. The night ended uneventfully, and I didn't hear from him over the weekend.

While walking to class the following Tuesday, Preston fell in step beside me. "I enjoyed the date party," he said softly, with that bright smile. I stared at him, not sure what to say. I was confused as to why he hadn't texted me, but I was also intrigued by how genuine his comment seemed. Before I had time to form my next sentence, he said, "We should get lunch sometime." My eyes widened, and I looked down. "Lunch?" I thought. "I didn't hear from this guy after our first date, and now he's asking me out again?" Preston continued, "Or dinner. We should get dinner." Before I knew it, I nodded and said, "Sure, that would be nice." A few days later, he texted me and invited me to dinner.

Our first date was the most awkward night of my life. Preston had been on dates here and there, but he'd never really had a girlfriend before. It wasn't because he wasn't cool. He was an athlete and a leader in his fraternity, and he was pretty good-looking, not that I'm biased or anything. Plenty of girls were interested in going out with him. But our first dates were extremely awkward, far from the romantic tales you read about in the storybooks.

Another fact that will help put the beginning of our relationship in perspective is that I'd ended a whirlwind relationship, which was everything I'd ever dreamed of, just a few months before Preston asked me out. It was a completely romantic, sweep-you-off-your-feet type of relationship. When it ended abruptly, I was crushed.

The beginning of my relationship with Preston was completely different. Our first meal together was at a local restaurant called Qdoba, which serves Mexican food in buffet style. It's like the Subway of Mexican food. I remember ordering nachos as I went down the line ahead of Preston. Because nachos are a quick meal to prepare, I moved quickly to the cash register. Preston's quesadilla took a bit longer to prepare, so I found myself alone in front of the cashier, who posed the impossible question: "Is this together or separate?"

"I don't know," I responded honestly.

She looked at me with both confusion and concern. "What do you mean you don't know?"

"Ma'am," I said as politely as I could muster, "I don't know."

"Are you on a date?"

"I don't know if I'm on a date."

"Well, you better just pay for your meal."

Thinking she was probably right, I got out my credit card and paid for my meal. Preston and I found our seats and had an hour-long conversation. During our entire time together, Preston never once mentioned that he hadn't paid for my meal.

We joke about this now, but I almost gave up on him several times. I was convinced he wasn't interested in me because this relationship was completely different than every other relationship that I had had before. For instance, we watched a movie in his dorm room one night and I joked that there was enough room for the Father, the Son, and the Holy Spirit on the couch between us. Thankfully, I had some good mutual friends who kept encouraging me not to give up on him.

What eventually made me fall in love with Preston Bell was our conversations about Jesus. Now, I'd had plenty of conversations in the past with people I was dating about Jesus, but the conversations with Preston were different. He didn't talk about faith because faith in Christ was a topic I liked to talk about. He talked about faith because he had an authentic relationship with Jesus and couldn't help but talk about Him. So, I stuck it out through the awkward early days, and Preston eventually asked me to be his girlfriend.

Preston later told me that he had prayed, read a book on marriage, and decided he would marry me when he asked me to be his girlfriend. From that point forward, he loved me with a steady and consistent love—a thrilling and exciting love bursting with the expectation of a lifetime of loving each other—a love that has deeply blessed me over the last ten years.

Our relationship wasn't perfect by any means. Like most relationships, ours struggled at times, but it differed from any other relationship I'd been in. It was much more in line with how God desired a dating relationship to be. This difference didn't come from me but was a result of Preston's leading. I didn't even know a relationship like this was possible because it was so different from everything our culture says about dating. I am so grateful to Preston's parents for raising him to value honoring God above the culture around him. It has served us both well.

Preston and I have now been married for almost ten years. Our sweet family has grown from two to three with the birth of our daughter, and our most recent life change entailed moving into a new house. If there's one thing I've learned from the moving process, it's that I have way too much stuff. While going through our things, I found some old memory boxes. Memory boxes are where you stick everything that you think will be important to you in the future—those things you can't throw away but don't want to display, so you stick them in a box and put them under your bed or in the attic.

I guess I'm a sucker for nostalgia because I have a lot of memory boxes. I began looking through a particular memory box from my late high school/early college years. Among the old photographs and awards were my old prayer journals. As I read through some of them, I was shocked at how much my thoughts hinged on the guys I had dated or had been interested in. None of them became my husband, but boy, did I ever think that they would!

I could feel the anguish and desire in my former self as I read through the things that I had written. It pains me to think about how much time I wasted pining after these guys that I haven't seen or thought about or talked to in years. They have no importance to my life right now.

As I sat on the floor, prayer journals sprawled open, I could picture the Lord in heaven looking at me, seeing me, and loving me, knowing that He had Preston for me the whole time. How I wish I could get back some of those hours. How I wish I had spent that time focusing on my relationship with Jesus, growing and becoming the woman that my husband deserved to meet.

This is a concept that I like to call emotional purity, saving not only your physical self but your emotional self for the Lord. My husband did this. I was his first female best friend, and it has proven to be such a blessing to our marriage over the years. While it was awkward in the beginning, the secureness of a relationship built on a solid foundation has allowed us to share love and romance blessed by God.

What ideas do you have in your head about what a dating relationship should look like? What about marriage? How do you think God's ideas about romantic relationships differ from the concept given to us by the world, not only sexually but emotionally as well? While the Bible doesn't speak specifically about our modern concept of dating (because it didn't exist in the time that it was written), it speaks plenty about matters of the heart.

Jesus is clear about the order in which we are supposed to seek things in our lives. In his first public sermon, Jesus told the crowds in Matthew 6:33, "Seek first the kingdom of God and his righteousness, and all these things will be added to you." In other words, seek Jesus and His kingdom above anything else. If asked, I think most of us would say, yes, our relationship with Jesus is most important to us. But ask yourself this: What do your thoughts tend to focus on? What do you worry about? What do you talk about? How do you spend your time?

Questions like these uncover what's most important in our lives. My high school prayer journals revealed that Jesus may not have been as high of a priority for me as I thought. We sometimes like to exclude romantic relationships or dating interests from this conversation, but we can't afford to do that. Throughout His teaching, Jesus emphasized the importance of putting God the Father first in our lives. Nothing is exempt from this, not even our date nights.

When we begin a romantic relationship with someone and expect them to be the sole source of our joy, we end up disappointed and they end up feeling a pressure that they were never meant to carry. This is true even in marriage. I have to put Jesus before my family so I can love and serve my family well.

So, what am I saying? Simply this. When it comes to dating relationships, put Jesus first. If you're single, put Jesus first. If you're engaged, put Jesus first. In your marriage, put Jesus first. Strive to think about Jesus more than you think about the person you're in a relationship with. Try giving Jesus the first moments of your day. Maybe you reach for your Bible before you reach for your phone in the morning, even if it's just five minutes. Converse with Jesus before you send that first text in the morning. Simple steps help us set priorities.

When talking about relationships, one of my Bible study leaders used to always say, "If we are both looking up at Jesus, we can't help but bump into each other." She would encourage us as young women to put our focus on Jesus, train our eyes on Him, not on any guy that walked our way. As a wife, in a committed relationship to Preston, I absolutely need to look at him and his needs, but he is also to look at mine (Phil. 2). When we are both looking to one another's needs, we can focus our attention on Christ together.

If you're in a relationship that seems a little out of order, it's never too late to make some changes. Like the woman at the well, Jesus sees your relationships and desires that your connections would honor Him and bring Him joy. That's the beautiful thing about Jesus, it's never too late. He wants to redeem our relationships. Relationships are a meaningful aspect of life that God designed for us to enjoy. Seek Jesus first in all your relationships and the joy of the Lord will be added to your life in abundance.

When Jesus instructs us to "seek first the kingdom of God and his righteousness, and all these things will be added to you," this includes cheer. **When we chase cheer in things outside of Jesus, we end up disappointed.** Relationships are a good thing, a really good thing that God designed for us to enjoy when they're in the right order. Who are you seeking?

UNEXPECTED FORGIVENESS

One habit crucial to navigating relationships is found in the way Jesus models how to extend and receive forgiveness. The verses that immediately precede Jesus's words in John 16:33 provide remarkable insight into Jesus's heart as it concerns relationships. During this conversation, the disciples declare their belief in Jesus as the Son of God. "Do you now believe?" Jesus responds. "The hour is coming, indeed it has come, when you will be scattered, each to his own home, and will leave me alone."

This response from Jesus always gives me pause. He drops this comment and then abruptly moves on. How did the disciples feel when they heard Jesus say this to them? Surely, they thought, "No! Not me! I won't leave him." Or "He must be talking about that guy, not me!" What I find fascinating about this part of their conversation is how Jesus kept going. He doesn't get hung up or stay stuck on the fact that all His friends, His closest followers, were going to desert Him.

Think about it: If you knew your best friend in the world was going to betray you and leave you stranded in your most dire time of need, would you keep on being friends with her? Would you keep investing in the relationship? What is remarkable about this passage is that it reveals how deep and real the forgiveness of Jesus is. He knew that His disciples would abandon Him, and yet He still loved them, walked with them, and remained in community with them until what He said came true. Even then, He loved them and desired them to return to Him.

In his commentary on the book of John, William Barclay writes, "He knew that his friends would abandon him, yet at the moment he did not reproach them, and afterwards he did not hold it against them. He loved human beings in all their weakness; saw them and loved them as they were" (Barclay 2017, 137).

Just as Jesus loved His disciples and the woman at the well, He loves us. In the same way He loved His disciples, we are to love one another. Jesus gives us this instruction, "Love one another: just as I have loved you" (John 13:34) and the Apostle Paul reminds us to "forgiv[e] each other, *just as* in Christ God forgave you" (Eph. 4:32, NIV).

Barclay argues that a key to the type of forgiveness Jesus displayed was that He saw human beings as they were. In other words, He had realistic expectations. "Love must be clear-sighted," Barclay comments (p.237). We set ourselves up for disappointment when we expect perfection from those with whom we are in a relationship. I find that this is often the case in my marriage. Without realizing it, I often put unrealistic expectations on my husband, and I end up setting myself up for disappointment that wasn't warranted or necessary.

Our ability to extend forgiveness is directly correlated to our understanding of the forgiveness we've received. Forgiving just as Jesus has forgiven us requires that we understand the depth of the forgiveness we've received. As King David writes in Psalm 103:

The Lord is merciful and gracious, slow to anger and abounding in steadfast love. He will not always chide, nor will he keep

> his anger forever. He does not deal with us according to our
> sins, nor repay us according to our iniquities. For as high as
> the heavens are above the earth, so great is his steadfast love
> toward those who fear him; as far as the east is from the west, so
> far does he remove our transgressions from us. (Ps. 103:8–12)

Those who understand they have been forgiven much, can extend much forgiveness to others. Sometimes, pride can take root in our hearts and make us forget how much we needed Jesus's forgiveness. Forgiveness and cheer are both rooted in love. Both are an understanding of the depth of God's love for us and our willingness to share that love with others, even those who have hurt us in the past. At the very beginning of the farewell discourse, in John 13:35 Jesus says, "People will know that you are my disciples, if you have love for one another."

Harboring unforgiveness can cheat us of cheer in our relationships. Whether it's our romantic relationships, familial relationships, friendships, or work relationships, unforgiveness is the thief that keeps on stealing. God desires for our relationships to bring us true joy from heaven. The enemy desires for us to stay angry and bitter.

Take inventory of your relationships. What do you notice? Are there any relationships that need a little extra attention? Invite Jesus to show you how to move forward. His desire is for your connections not to create confusion, but to bring you cheer.

 Cheer Practice

5—Breath Prayers

Pray this scripture on an inhale and exhale.

- Inhale: one, two, three, four
- Exhale: five, six, seven, eight

Try breathing and meditating on the words or saying the words aloud on those counts.

- Inhale: Love each other
- Exhale: as I have loved you
  (John 13:34)

- Inhale: Forgive each other
- Exhale: as God has forgiven you
  (Eph. 4:32)

6—Scripture Callout

Memorizing scripture is such an important part of practicing the presence of God.

Our fourth callout:

Seek first the kingdom of God and his righteousness, and all these things will be added to you. (Matt. 6:33)

Practice saying this verse out loud, repeat it, write it down, and put it somewhere that you can see it.

7—Gratitude Challenge

I believe that gratitude is the best prescription for cheerfulness. When we think about the things we are grateful for, it is hard to stay focused on our challenging circumstances. Thankfulness is not always something that comes natural to us. We have to practice.

I encourage you to write down three things that you are grateful for today. This could be in relation to what we've studied in this chapter or just related to something in your life right now. I encourage you to think of something different from the last chapter.

Thank you, Jesus, for:

_____

_____

_____

8—Spread Some Cheer

A simple way to choose cheer in our lives is to share cheer with others.

TODAY'S CHEER CHALLENGE:
MAKE A NEW CONNECTION!

In this chapter, we discussed our relationships—the good, the bad, and the joyful. Look around and see who in your sphere of influence needs a friend and make a new connection. My daughter recently began a new preschool program. On the first day at Meet the Teacher, we walk into the classroom and are greeted by her new teachers. There was an awkwardness in the room as no one really knows each other. I looked around the room and took a deep breath, and whispered, "Okay, Lord, I'll go first." I walked over to one of the parents and said, "Hi, I'm Nicolet and this is Josie, it's nice to meet you." The parent's eyes brightened, and a smile came across their lips as they returned the greeting and then struck up the conversation. Sometimes making a new connection can look like going first. Not being afraid to simply introduce yourself to someone new and get to know them. Where is an area in your life that you could practice that this week? Maybe there's someone in your office who you've not interacted with or perhaps you've spoken to them as you walk past their desk but have never really taken the time to get to know them. Ask God to show you who you can connect with this week.

FIVE

Comparison

I t's a Monday night, and I'm sitting on my couch with a million things I should be doing. Instead, I'm scrolling. It's innocent at first. My finger finds and clicks open the app automatically, before I even realize what's happening. "Aww, that looks fun!" I think as I observe a picture of my friend enjoying some time at the beach. I swipe left. "Oh! That's such a cute swimsuit! None of my swimsuits are that cute." Before I know it, my finger has closed out of Instagram and opened my Target app. I find three swimsuits and add them to my cart.

The Target box with my new suits arrives on my porch three days later. Excitedly I unbox my new purchases. But when I try them on, they're too tight and hit me in all the wrong places. Looking in the mirror, I realize I don't look nearly as cute as my friend on Instagram. Buyer remorse hits hard and fast. Why did I feel compelled to purchase three new suits? I don't have a pool, and I have no plans to go to the beach anytime soon. Also, I need to lose several pounds, so it isn't the ideal time for me to buy swimsuits. But now, here I am with three swimsuits that must be returned. On top of that, I now have thoughts of a negative body image and a strong sense of lack or missing out for not being at the beach.

It's Thursday afternoon now, and Josie and I are having a playdate at a friend's house. Their kids have a dreamy playroom with many cool things that are all neatly organized. As I look around and see Josie playing with these toys in their beautiful space, suddenly our cabinet full of toys doesn't seem like enough. Our house doesn't seem big enough. My sweet friend hasn't said a word to make these thoughts come, but they come, and they build.

Our playdate ends. I get in my car, back out of the driveway, and think, "My car isn't as new or as big as hers." Pulling up to my house, I feel like it isn't enough. I'm experiencing completely different feelings from when I left my home a few hours before, and I'm certainly not thinking about the thatched roof houses and dirt floors I witnessed in Nicaragua a few months before on a mission trip.

Can you find yourself in these stories? Do you ever have these thoughts and wonder where they come from or how your attitude could change so fast? "Am I enough?" is a question we often ask—whether we like it or not. This brings us to our third "C" that cheats us from cheerfulness: *Comparison.*

Comparison is sneaky and often subconscious. The pressure of comparing ourselves with others is compounded by the time spent on our phones and computers. I recently read a quote by

Theodore Roosevelt that says, "Comparison is the thief of joy." (Roosevelt 1905). This quote has been on my mind for the past few months, and I believe it holds much truth.

Our joy is often stolen by our lack of contentment. Most often, our lack of contentment comes from comparing ourselves to others. What can we do about it? Fortunately, the Bible addresses this issue. Something I love about the Bible is that its words are living and active. The Holy Spirit speaks into our lives through the words of scripture with the same power and wisdom He spoke to those who first received it.

One instance where the Bible speaks to comparison is found in Paul's letter to Galatia, "For am I now seeking the approval of man, or of God? Or am I trying to please man? If I were still trying to please man, I would not be a servant of Christ" (Gal. 1:10).

Comparison is rooted in our desire to want to be like or not to be like others. When thinking about comparison, a good question to ask ourselves is, "Who am I trying to please?" When we feel inadequate or like we are not enough, we can ask ourselves the question: To whom are we looking for approval? According to Paul, we cannot please people and God. This echoes the words of Jesus in Matthew 6:24, "No one can serve two masters."

That's another convicting thought. When we compare ourselves to those around us, we allow them to be masters over us. We invite them in and give them a seat in the front of our minds. This isn't easy for us to admit. We don't like to think that anyone or anything could have power over us, but our innermost thoughts can reveal a lot about us. Consider what thoughts persistently cross your mind when you aren't actively thinking. What keeps you awake at night? Maybe you can relate to having thoughts like:

"Is so-and-so mad at me? Why was she acting weird around me today?"

"Why hasn't he texted me back?"

"Ugh. That outfit is so cute. My outfits are never that cute."

"My daughter doesn't have that new toy."

"I wish I could go on that vacation."

You can fill in the blank with your thoughts. When you notice your thoughts sounding like this, ask yourself, "Who am I trying to please?"

Maybe you experience feelings of inadequacy about your life, thinking it doesn't measure up to the look of other people's lives. Or maybe your life has the outward appearance of perfection, but your marriage is in shambles. Maybe you would win best dressed at the party, but your heart is empty and void. Wherever you find yourself, scripture shows us another way:

So we do not lose heart. Though our outer self is wasting away, our inner self is being renewed day by day. For this light momentary affliction is preparing for us an eternal weight of glory beyond all comparison, as we look **not** to the things that are seen but to the things that are unseen. For the things that are seen are transient, but the things that are unseen are eternal." (2 Cor. 4:16–18)

The phrase here, "we do not lose heart," mirrors the phrase "take heart!" in John 16:33. Which is also translated as "Be of Good Cheer!" It would be accurate for us to paraphrase this scripture: "So we do not lose our cheer . . . because we know what is coming!"

Scripture has something to say about the comparison culture we find ourselves in. Paul says, "You want to compare? Go ahead! I promise; nothing will compare to the eternal weight of glory waiting for you!" According to Paul, the key is to fix our eyes on what is *unseen*, not on what is seen. The things that are seen will waste away, but the things that are unseen will last forever. Perfect houses, decorations, wardrobes, and everything else we can see are temporary. We are not to fix our eyes, direct our focus, or spend all our time on these things.

THE ENEMY OF ENVY

I had lunch with my friend recently and she talked about how she had been reading Genesis and what God was teaching her about envy. She confessed the way that the stories of Genesis and beyond in the Bible had convicted her of envy in her own life. When she first started talking, I had the thought, "Envy isn't really something I struggle with." As she continued speaking, I became increasingly aware of the extent to which envy is a challenge for me. I had just called it something different that sounded nicer and made me feel better. The more I listened to my friend, the more I knew what I had labeled "comparison" was a deeper problem of envy.

Envy is ever-present in scripture from beginning to end. The more I thought about it, the more I recognized that wherever there's a story of envy in scripture, comparison is close by. In Genesis 3, Eve envied what she didn't have. She saw what God had and desired it. She compared what she had to what He had, which resulted in feelings of envy, and the actions that followed were detrimental.

When Sarah grew impatient, she took matters into her own hands and made a mess of things. She planned for Abraham to sleep with Sarah's servant, Hagar. Hagar conceived a son, Ishmael, and soon, Sarah and Hagar entered a vicious cycle of comparison and envy. A few years later, Sarah bore a son, Isaac, just as God had promised. Conflict and jealousy were key features of the boys' relationship as well.

Skipping ahead to the New Testament, the religious leaders were envious of Jesus. They were envious of the way the crowds followed Him and the power He displayed. They were power-hungry and wanted to be in control. Comparing themselves to Jesus and allowing that to grow into envy led to them plotting to kill Jesus. Their envy prevented them from truly knowing Jesus, benefiting from His teachings, and embracing His love. Despite His invitation, they turned Him away.

Jesus's first cousin, John the Baptist, could have easily fallen into the trap of comparison and envy like these religious leaders. Both John and Jesus were the result of miraculous pregnancies;

they were each filled with the Spirit from a young age and were both born for very specific roles.

My daughter was born three months after my niece. I often have to stop myself from comparing the two of them. I compare milestones and sometimes worry that Josie is behind or missing out on something. Josie feels it too. She often tells me she wants something her cousin has that she doesn't. I wonder if this is something Mary and Elizabeth would have experienced.

On the other hand, the sweet thing about our daughters being so close in age is that they are built-in best friends. They are precious. They love each other so much. I imagine this is something that Jesus and John experienced, since they were so close in age and had a unique relationship.

John was prophesied to have a very specific role before his birth: to "prepare the way for the Lord" (Isa. 40:3). When John set about this work, he began to draw crowds. People wondered, "Is he the Messiah?" or "Is he a prophet?" One day, as John was baptizing outside of Bethany, a group of religious leaders questioned him about whether he was the Messiah.

John answered quickly, "I am not the Christ." They persisted, asking, "Are you Elijah? A prophet?" (The Jewish people believed that Elijah would return before the coming of the Messiah.) John answered, "No." They pressed further, "Who are you? We need to give an answer to those who sent us. What do you say about yourself?" (John 1:22). John replied:

"I am the voice of one crying out in the wilderness, 'Make straight the way of the Lord.' as the prophet Isaiah told" (John 1:23).

Unsatisfied with his answer, they fired back, "Then why are you baptizing?" John replied that while he baptized with water, there was one among them that they didn't yet know "even he who comes after me, the strap of whose sandal I am not worthy to untie" (John 1:27).

The magnitude of this statement can be lost on us modern-day readers pretty quickly. Untying sandals was work reserved for slaves, and believe me, it was not pleasant work. Only the elite had access to small carriages and horses; therefore, traveling on foot was the most common mode of transportation. They couldn't jump in their car or on the subway to get where they were going. Roads were dusty and likely to be covered in animal waste. Feet were filthy! Commentator William Barclay writes,

> There was a Rabbinic saying which said that a disciple might do for his master anything that a servant did, **except** only to untie his sandals. That was too menial a service for even a disciple to render." (Barclay 2017, 93)

This gives us better context for what John is saying to the religious leaders about his role and the role of Jesus. John is clear from the outset that he is only a voice calling out and preparing the way. But there is one who is coming who is greater than anything you can imagine.

The continual comparison of John and Jesus by those who were curious was a source of tension for John. However, John remained faithful to his calling and consistently pointed to Jesus as the greater one.

DO YOU LIKE TO COME IN SECOND PLACE?

My dad, a longtime high school football coach, is extremely competitive. I'll never forget our conversation following one of my high school tennis matches, where I hit a girl in the face with the ball. (Let's just say that my reason for playing tennis was more about staying in shape than because I was good at it.)

When I hit her, I immediately ran up to the net and apologized. I felt so bad! After the match, my dad pulled me aside and said, "Nic, why did you apologize to that girl?" I responded, "Daddy, I smoked her in the face! I felt terrible! I didn't mean to hit her." He rolled his eyes and laughed, knowing that when it came to sports, I didn't inherit his competitive streak.

On the other hand, when it came to academic performance and school activities, my Daddy's competitive streak came out in me. I didn't want to be second when it came to grades or involvement. This carried over into college and into the workplace. I desire to do everything I do at 110 percent. And if I can be honest with you, I secretly desire to be the best at everything I do. I want to be the best wife, the best student pastor, the best business owner, and the best family member. I don't love second place. Ouch. Admitting that one hurts, but can you relate?

A few chapters later, in John 3, John's disciples get jealous. Before Jesus began his public ministry, crowds flocked to John and his disciples. So when Jesus enters the scene, John's disciples say, "Hey! Everyone is going over there to be baptized by Jesus! No one is coming over here anymore!" In our language: "Hey! That guy is getting all of the follows/likes! No one is interested in what I am doing or what I am saying, everyone is paying attention to Him!" In our culture, where attention and fame equal happiness and second place is just not good enough, we can definitely relate to how John's disciples were feeling.

John's response to his disciples is one of a true follower of Christ. He knew his place and he knew his role. He said, "Guys, you heard me talk about how Jesus was greater than me. You heard me say that I was preparing the way for Him, that I was baptizing with water, but that He would baptize with the Holy Spirit." In other words, John is saying, "I'm not jealous at all!" In fact, "this joy of mine is now complete!" He concludes with one of my favorite verses in all of scripture: "He must increase, but I must decrease" (John 3:29–30). In a situation where John should have been jealous and upset, he resisted. He chose to put Jesus above himself. He knew his role and found joy in it. He submitted to the authority of Jesus and his joy was made *complete*.

What about your own life? Are you still joyful when all the attention is taken away from you? To whom do you compare yourself? Often, we try to find joy by being the center of attention and being recognized or acknowledged for our hard work. We don't like the spotlight to be taken away from us. We can find fleeting joy (or temporary happiness) in attention and applause, but we're left empty and incomplete at the end of the day.

John was okay with second place. John's joy was made complete by understanding his position and purpose and lifting up the name of Jesus. John was confident in his role and as a result he found his confidence and joy in his Savior. In the same way, our joy is made complete when we take a surrendered posture before Jesus and desire to increase His name and fame and decrease our own.

So, I confessed to you my competitive nature and desire to be the best at what I do. When I look at my heart, I know that this is an area that the Lord wants to work on. Scripture tells us that God calls us to work wholeheartedly at whatever we do as if we are serving Him and not man (Col. 3:23). This elicits my best effort. But if I desire to *be* the best instead of *giving* my best to God, I have missed the point. If I try to be the best, I will continually strive and search, trying to find fulfillment in the attention in the praise of others.

Receive this lesson from John today. Through the power of the Holy Spirit, may we release jealousy, envy, and bitterness, and instead, cheer for the way God is working in the lives of others. Let's be quick to put His glory on display instead of our own. When we recognize our role, our joy can be made complete.

Jesus knew His role and modeled this for us:

Have this mind among yourselves, which is yours in Christ Jesus, who, though he was in the form of God, did not count equality with God a thing to be grasped, but emptied himself, by taking the form of a servant, being born in the likeness of

men. And being found in human form, he humbled himself
by becoming obedient to the point of death. (Phil. 2:5–8)

If Jesus—the only one who had the right to be the best and the
only one who had the right to stand in first place—humbled
himself, how much more should we humble ourselves to Him?
The most beautiful thing about knowing our role is that when
we submit to Jesus, we enter into freedom, life, and joy. James
4:10 promises that when you "humble yourselves before the
Lord, . . . he will lift you up." In fact, we find more joy in second
place than in first.

AUTHENTIC VS. PERFORMATIVE

Not only should we guard ourselves from the trap of comparing
ourselves to others, but we also have a responsibility to the way
we present ourselves. Are we presenting only the best parts of
our lives, or are we presenting the most authentic version of
ourselves? How are we presenting ourselves not only on social
media but also in our day-to-day relationships with others? We
can ask ourselves: Am I posting that picture to make others
think I have it all together, or am I posting to share the joy of
my family's life? I love a photographer-grade picture as much as
anyone, and I don't think there is anything wrong with sharing
that, but I think it is essential that we ask ourselves—what is the
motive behind our sharing? We don't want to invite others into
comparison; we want to encourage and build up those around us.

As followers of Jesus, we have a responsibility to authenticity. When considering my desire to be the best, I think of Matthew 6:1 in the Message translation, where Jesus says, "Be especially careful when you are trying to be good so that you don't make a performance out of it. It might be good theater, but the God who made you won't be applauding." I desire to be authentic, not performative. Our attempts at perfection do not fool God. He sees our hearts, minds, and all the details of our lives, and He loves us anyway.

Jesus didn't present a perfect persona. Although He was the only perfect person ever to live, He lived poor and humble. Jesus was never anything but Himself. He didn't change His personality or persona based on the group of people He was with. He didn't concern himself with impressing the Pharisees. Jesus was content and genuine to His core, inviting us to live the same.

Several examples come to mind when I think about a life of contentment. First, I think about my sister. She models this beautifully as she lives a life not concerned with "keeping up with the Jones." She is my biological cousin, but she came to live with our family when I was just four years old. I have had a front-row seat as she experienced her share of great hardship, and over time, has allowed Jesus to use those hardships to make her value what is essential in life. I also have witnessed her pass this down to her three teenage children.

Second, I think about my experiences on mission trips to Central America. One particular memory stands out to me from a recent trip where we visited the home of a precious older woman.

As we entered her house, she was sweeping her floor. The home had four simple cinder block walls, one open room, a thatched roof, and a dirt floor. Tears sprang to my eyes as I watched the woman sweeping her dirt floor. I thought about all the times I complained about vacuuming or mopping my own floor. She was just moving the dust around, but she was content and took pride in what little she had. I don't fully know what hardship this woman had faced over the years, but the hunch in her back and the limp in her right leg told pieces of her story. The light in her eyes shared another part of her story: She had joy despite her circumstances. Many Americans would look at this woman and pity her for having so little, but in this moment I looked at her and I envied her. I possessed more material things than she did, but she possessed more joy and peace than I did.

Words fall short in describing contentment. Reflecting on this, I realized that contentment is not something you can adequately describe; it is something to behold. Contentment is something that you experience in a life fully yielded to Jesus. Contentment is the secret weapon to combat comparison and increase our cheer.

FAKE LIFE ALARM

One evening, several years ago, I was sitting on the couch, curled up, watching a movie while also scrolling on my phone. I caught myself getting swept up in the story, as well as what I was viewing on my phone. Before I knew it, my marriage began to seem subpar because, unlike the husband in the movie who had cleaned the house, cooked dinner, and put the kids to bed, my husband still put his socks on the floor RIGHT NEXT TO THE HAMPER. I compared my life to the scene I was watching and felt sorry for myself!

I yelled, "FAKE LIFE!" at the exact moment Preston walked into the living room. He burst into laughter and asked me what in the world I was talking about. Since then, the "Fake Life!" alarm has become an ongoing joke between Preston and me. Whenever we start to get caught up in comparison or in the things that we know are unimportant, one of us will sound the alarm and say, "Fake Life! Fake Life!" Through this silly joke, the Lord has helped us to realize when we are sliding down the slippery slope of comparison.

However, this reminder is not a sad one for us. "We do not lose our cheer" because we have been given a "Real Life!" that is far more abundant than anything we could imagine (John 10:10; Eph. 3:20). No, I'm not perfectly dressed, but Jesus has "clothed me with the garments of salvation, he has cover me with the robe of righteousness" (Isa. 61:10). Yes, we sometimes struggle to get to the grocery store and get dinner on the table. Still, we know we are invited to the greatest feast of all time (Rev. 19:9).

Even huge struggles are "light and momentary afflictions" according to the apostle Paul, who went through immense real-life suffering. Let us untangle ourselves from the trap of comparison by letting our gratitude move us to a place of generosity. Our reality, our "Real Life," is found in the Presence of Jesus, and in His presence is the fullness of Joy (Ps. 16:11).

So, if we compare, let's do so as the scriptures encourage us—with eternity in mind.

 Cheer Practice

5—Breath Prayers

Pray this scripture on an inhale and exhale.

- Inhale: one, two, three, four
- Exhale: five, six, seven, eight

Try breathing and meditating on the words or saying the words aloud on those counts.

- Inhale: He has wrapped me
- Exhale: with a robe of righteousness
  (Isa. 61:10)

- Inhale: He must increase
- Exhale: I must decrease
  (John 3:30)

6—Scripture Callout

Up until this point, we've worked on memorizing four short scriptures together. I'm going to push us a little bit this week for a little longer scripture passage. This is one

of the very first passages I memorized when I was a teen-
ager and it still repeats in my mind often today.

Our fifth callout:

> Have the same mindset of Christ Jesus: Who, being in the very
> nature God, did not consider equality with God something
> to be used to his own advantage; rather, he made himself
> nothing by taking the very nature of a servant. . . . (Phil. 2:5–7)

Practice saying this verse out loud, repeat it, write it
down, and put it somewhere that you can see it.

7—Gratitude Challenge

I believe that gratitude is the best prescription for cheerfulness. When we think about the things we are grateful
for, it is hard to stay focused on our challenging circumstances. Thankfulness is not always something that comes
natural to us. We have to practice.

I encourage you to write down three things that you are
grateful for today. This could be in relation to what we've
studied in this chapter or just related to something in your
life right now. I encourage you to think of something different from the last chapter.

Thank you, Jesus, for:

_____

_____

_____

8—Spread Some Cheer

A simple way to choose cheer in our lives is to share cheer with others.

TODAY'S CHEER CHALLENGE:
COMPLIMENT SOMEONE!

Throughout this chapter, we talked about comparison. One of the easiest ways to overcome comparison is contentment. When you can genuinely give someone a compliment without feelings of jealousy, this is spreading cheer. Slow down at the grocery store and look your clerk in the eye. I often say things like, "You have the brightest smile" or "Your eyes are a beautiful blue." It's always amazing to see their response and watch their expression change as they realize they are truly being seen. It can be to someone random, or it could be to someone close to you. I'll sometimes remind myself to slow down and look at Preston and tell him something I love about him that I often overlook. Or perhaps it's telling my child's teacher at drop off or a coworker, "That's such a cute dress!" This is a simple way to spread cheer that is often overlooked because of the busy pace we keep. Intentionally think of ways you can give genuine compliments today.

SIX

Control

When Josie was just over a year old, we visited my parents at their house in the country. I sat on the back porch and watched my parents blow bubbles with my little girl. Instead of watching for new bubbles, Josie focused on the bubbles that had already passed by her, straining her neck to see them. All the while, my parents shouted, "Josie! Josie, come here!" to catch her attention and direct her gaze toward a new group of sparkling bubbles that waited for her. But Josie was too caught up. She continued staring at and chasing the bubbles that had already passed her.

As I watched this, I realized how easily I can get distracted and focus on the wrong things. How often does God call out, "Nicolet! Nicolet! Over here!!" but I'm stuck, straining my neck, looking in the wrong direction, fixated on what is behind me or what is coming next instead of what's right in front of me?

I wonder how often we miss what God is doing in our present because we are too focused on the past or the future. Scripture teaches us to be focused on the moment—this day—the Lord has given us. Jesus tells His followers in Matthew 6:34, "Therefore, do not be anxious about tomorrow, for tomorrow will be anxious for itself. Today has enough trouble of its own."

This doesn't mean we can't make plans. I'm a planner! But it means we make our plans with an open hand, willing and ready to change or adapt as the Lord leads us. The Message translation puts it like this:

> Give your entire attention to what God is doing right now, and don't get worked up about what may or may not happen tomorrow. God will help you deal with whatever hard things come up when the time comes." (Matt. 6:34, MSG)

We like to be in control, don't we? However, we can't be in control and allow Jesus to be in control at the same time.

Choosing Cheer includes focusing on the present instead of staying stuck in the past or straining toward the future—looking for the next accomplishment or pining away for the next stage of life. When I finish college, when I get married, when I get the right job, when I get the right house, *then* I will be able to focus on Jesus. Staying focused in the past could look like living in shame or regret, or longing for good days gone by. Thinking, "If only I could go back and change this," or "Those were the best days." Your life is happening now, not later and not in the past. Jesus wants us to experience the fullness of His joy NOW.

We often overcomplicate God's will, which is simple: Seek Him above everything else.

A great example of this is found in the early church. As a part of his calling, the Apostle Paul took many missionary journeys to spread the good news of Jesus Christ and build the kingdom of God. In Acts 16, we read that Paul and his team of missionaries began making their way to Asia but were "forbidden by the Holy Spirit to speak the word in Asia." So, they "attempted to go into Bythnia, but the Spirit of Jesus did not allow them" (Acts 16:7). What bugs me about this passage is that the author of Acts, most likely the apostle Luke, doesn't give us any details here. I want to ask him: How did the Holy Spirit forbid them? Was it a physical roadblock? Did they hear a voice from heaven? How was he so sure that the Holy Spirit was saying the things He was saying? Why would the Spirit not want the Good News shared in these areas? Luke doesn't spell out how Paul knew the Spirit was not allowing them to enter those areas, but Luke does give us a few more details on how Paul knew where to go instead.

> A vision appeared to Paul in the night: a man of Macedonia was standing there urging him and saying, "Come over to Macedonia and help us." And when Paul had seen the vision, immediately we sought to go into Macedonia, concluding that God had called us to preach the gospel to them. (Acts 16:9–10)

The Spirit moves and directs Paul and his companions in this passage. Paul doesn't seem surprised when the Spirit changes his plans. Paul had an agenda and a plan but was willing to change them in response to the Spirit's leading. Although I wish we had more details about how the Spirit led and directed Paul and his companions, we can conclude a couple of things that are helpful to us as we learn to walk in step with the Spirit.

First, it's very important to hold our plans with open hands. Sometimes, we get so attached to our plans and ideas of how things should be that we have difficulty letting go when God has something different in mind.

Second, Paul was actively listening and seeking the Spirit's guidance. While he waited for clear direction, he kept his head down and kept working. He continued to share the good news of Jesus, where he was until he was told to move or do something different.

Sometimes, we can become complacent or lazy when we feel like we aren't receiving clear direction from God. I have fallen into this trap many times. When we find ourselves in a season of uncertainty, unsure of where God is calling us or what we should be doing, it is important that we focus on the clear instructions that we have in scripture. Sharing Jesus with who is around us, caring for the needy, reading the Word, and praying are all clear instructions we have as followers of Jesus.

Sometimes we can get so focused on waiting for a dramatic leading or instruction from God in our lives that we skip over or underemphasize the clear instructions and commands He has already given us in His Word. For instance, we don't need a huge revelation from the Spirit to know we are called to care for the hungry. Jesus's teachings make it clear that serving and helping others is a call for all of His followers. Paul's story in Acts 16 shows us an example of active waiting—actively being about what God has made clear to us in His word while waiting on His specific leading or instruction.

We all desire to be in control in one way or another. We hold on tightly to things we can control, and we worry about the things we can't. Control affects how we approach all the other C's that can cheat us of our cheer. When we are focused on control, our joy is easily affected by our challenges, connections, and comparisons.

WAITING

My dad is from Pittsburgh, Pennsylvania. Once or twice a year, we would make long road trips from South Mississippi to visit my grandparents, aunts, and uncles in Pittsburgh. When I think about these childhood road trips, I think about stopping at rest areas and getting something out of the vending machine. I remember racing with my brother from our car to the vending machine, then standing there and thinking about what we wanted. This was a big decision! We would survey all of our options, and after finally making a decision, we would put in our money (yes, actual coins) and punch the letter-number combination to receive what we wanted.

On one occasion, I remember entering "A6" for M&M's. The machine came to life and began to shake and jolt. But, instead of heading toward row A, the grabber arm headed toward row C, settled on "C2," and gave us almonds! Almonds? We were so disappointed.

On another trip and another rest stop, we put our money in and waited patiently for the machine to start moving, only to get nothing in return. We stood there and waited, hoping for a miracle. But nothing moved. Nothing happened. I gave the vending machine a little shake. My brother gave it a little kick. We waited again. Still, nothing happened. We dug deep in our pockets and Mom's purse only to realize we had used our LAST seventy-five cents!

Prayer can feel like this. You tell God what you want, and sometimes you get it. Other times, you tell God what you want and get something you didn't ask for. And still other times, you tell God what you want, and it seems like you get nothing. You want to shake the vending machine, kick it, and raise your fists toward heaven in response to the silence.

These are the moments when waiting becomes challenging. What are we to do when we ask God for something but don't get an answer? Or maybe we get an answer, but it's not the answer we want? Maybe we get almonds instead of M&M's.

This is the most difficult part of waiting and not being in control. Paul's words in Philippians, "do not be anxious about anything, but in everything by prayer and supplication with thanksgiving," sound great when times are good, but what about when times are hard? What about in the face of tragedy or great loss? What about when we ask, and heaven seems to respond in silence? What do we do? How do we keep praying and showing up before God when we fear disappointment?

Perhaps you have a specific situation or circumstance in mind.

I know I do. This involves a deeply personal struggle. I alluded to this in the beginning of the book, but I want to go into a little more detail for this lesson. Preston and I walked through a season of over three years in which it seemed like I was knocking on the doors of heaven with my prayers, and heaven seemed to be responding in silence.

My husband and I have been married almost nine years. Right after we were married, we discovered a health condition that was not only affecting my everyday life, but also greatly threatening my fertility. After two surgeries, we were led to seek fertility treatment. To our great enthusiasm, with just a little bit of intervention, we were able to get pregnant very quickly. For the first three months, we were being monitored weekly by our fertility team. At a routine ultrasound, one where we were actually supposed to graduate from the fertility clinic and move over to the regular OBGYN, the doctor completed the ultrasound, and I saw her throat bobble. I could see the baby on the screen, but the baby was still. "Nicolet," she said, "I can't find a heartbeat."

We lost our first baby through a miscarriage, which led to my third surgery. I entered into a season of grief and confusion, mixed with physical pain to remind me of the emptiness in my womb. Months later, we completed our first round of IVF treatments. Coupled with a traumatic personal experience during these same few weeks, our first attempt at IVF was a complete failure, leading to no baby and a speculation that my eggs may not be able to produce a child.

Six months later, in March of 2020, as we prayed and believed God for a miracle, we began our second round of IVF treatments. Enter COVID-19. I was forced to stop treatments in the middle, which wreaked havoc on my body. Fast-forward to the beginning of May, we were finally able to begin our third round of IVF. By a miracle of God, we made it out with two embryos that would be tested to see if they could become a fetus. We waited. A mix up in the lab called for more waiting. Then we got the dreaded phone call. Neither of the embryos developed into babies, indicating a problem with my eggs.

This catapulted Preston and me into another round of intense grief and confusion. While most of our friends were having their second child, we were waiting. We did our best to continue to hope and believe that we, too, would get the chance to have a family. During this time, people would say, "Oh, you're young, you'll be fine!" And, on some days, I would be. On other days, I was far from fine. Can you relate? Have you asked God for a miracle only to get silence?

When we get silence, it's harder to pray, isn't it? It's harder to ask. I found myself thinking, "God isn't answering; is this God's will? What if my prayers are selfish? What if I'm praying for the wrong thing?"

I want to share an excerpt of something I wrote in my journal about two years into that season:

This prayer has still not yet been answered. This story isn't wrapped up and tied up with a pretty bow. In fact, an answer seems farther away than it has in years. It is a daily struggle to receive God's peace and rest BEFORE the answer comes. I began by thinking "When this is over, I'll rest." Well, push back after push back and 2 and ½ years later, I'm learning the hard way that we can't wait to find rest until the storm has passed. But that I serve a God who can and will speak Peace over my situation. That I serve a God who continually replaces my fear and anxiety with his peace and renewed hope. When we come to God in prayer, showing up and asking God again and again, we will receive God's peace. My prayer isn't answered, but I have the peace of Jesus. Not all the time, not perfectly, but I am working on receiving his peace.

This is what Jesus meant when he told us to pray, "Your Kingdom come, your will be done on earth as it is in heaven." We know this isn't how things were supposed to be. In heaven, we know there is no more sickness, no more pain, no more tears. . . . We surrender our will to God's will and our desires begin to line up with his desires.

I don't remember how long it took me to get to this point of surrender, but I remember the freedom I felt after I did. My entire perspective changed. It was as if I finally realized how tightly I was trying to hold on to control that I never truly possessed in the first place.

This is my story, or at least, a part of my story. This is what causes waves of doubt to try and fill my heart and mind. What is it for you? It doesn't matter how big or small your prayer may seem; it's not a competition. **God doesn't receive our prayers with a measuring stick. God sees every single one of your situations and he desires to speak his peace into it.** So what happens when our prayers aren't answered? God answers with His peace.

Our prayers aren't always pretty. Pretty prayers aren't normally honest prayers. Sometimes, they are gut-wrenching, ugly-crying, fist-pounding, snot-dripping, whole-hearted prayers.

Our prayer was answered, not in the way we expected, but even better. You've already read about my daughter in this book, so you can guess how this story ends. Josie Lou Bell, our miracle girl, was conceived three and a half years into our fertility journey with minimal intervention. She is proof that God is still working and healing in miraculous ways. She is proof that doctors don't have the final say on what God can and can't do. That's not to say we don't believe in the power of healing through medical care. My husband is a physician and has dedicated his life to it. But on many days, I look at her, tears fill my eyes, and I whisper, "Thank you, Jesus." I will never stop thanking Him for the miracle that she is.

As Paul and his companions modeled, let's hold our plans up to heaven with open hands, trusting that God is leading us and believing that His plans are better than anything we could imagine.

RELEASING CONTROL IN THE LITTLE THINGS

Because God has been faithful to me in many significant areas of my life, I find trusting Him with the big decisions easier. Lately, I've noticed that I am holding on to control in smaller areas in my life. Namely, how many toys were on the floor, that the toilet paper roll was left empty, and that I had already said the same thing three times. I had to release control in the journey to becoming a parent, and now I have to release control daily in the parenting journey. Controlling a three-year-old is an impossible task. While it is my job as her mother to lead her and to set boundaries for her, controlling her is not really an option. As I watch my three-year-old, I think about the teenagers and parents I have worked with over the years and the way we parents have a way of trying to control our children. I think about the drastic changes in our parenting and our children's lives from even one generation before us.

I remember my husband's father's story of growing up on the Mississippi Gulf Coast as one of four brothers. His dad, who we called Grandpa, would read stories to them at night, usually the Hardy Boys or The Adventures of Huckleberry Finn. Full of adventure as young boys, the brothers were motivated by their imaginations and pictured themselves as Tom Sawyer.

He recalls the day they were swimming in the bayou across the street, an activity their mother forbade, as it was a nasty, stagnant body of water. Midswim, they heard the large bell at the back door of their home. Their mother rang the bell to summon the boys when they were playing outside. When Grandpa gathered all the brothers, he gave them an exciting announcement—the family had won a raffle at the car wash. The prize was a small sailboat! The boat was red, with a mainsail and a jib. It was only twelve feet long, but to the boys, it was a yacht.

They named the sailboat Petite Rouge, meaning "little red." When each boy turned ten years old, their dad taught them how to sail the boat. After many days out on the water, my father-in-law and his oldest brother, Homer, were "approved" to sail the boat alone.

Outside the Gulfport harbor, buoys marked out an area not further south than channel Marker #2 and not east of Moses Pier. All of this was within the view of the upper deck of the Gulfport Yacht Club, where the boys' parents could keep an eye on them.

One beautiful day, my father-in-law took the boat out by himself. He reached the #2 Marker, the boundary his parents gave him. The wind out of the southwest was around eight knots, and as he looked south, he saw Cat Island. Barrier islands protect the Mississippi Coast. Cat Island is one of these islands, and there is nothing on the island but a nature reserve. As he looked at the island, he decided it looked close (although it lies east and west about six miles from Gulfport). Then, he channeled his inner Tom Sawyer, ignored the warnings of his mom and dad, and set out to conquer the voyage to Cat Island.

After about an hour and a half, he made it to the northeast beach of the island. The centerboard popped up as it contacted the sand in shallow water. He beached the boat, stepped out, and put his small bare feet on the sand. Then, he jumped right back in the boat and sailed straight back to the harbor, where his crying mother greeted him with a hug and then proceeded to discipline him—grounding him for the summer. Despite his mother's hysteria, he doesn't recall his dad being all that upset. We think Grandpa had a little bit of Tom Sawyer in him too.

Five years later, my father-in-law took another voyage to another barrier island. This time, he and his brother set their course to Chandeleur Island for an overnight campout. The weather looked clear, so they went on their way. They made it to the island and set up camp. They enjoyed an evening with the stars, the sea, and the sand, but as their eyes opened at the first crack of light, they knew something had changed.

Storm clouds were brewing in the distance, and they scurried to gather their supplies and get back in their boat. As they loaded the boat, they sensed that this was about to be bad. With no cover on the island, they decided to try to make it back. The winds picked up and began to toss them around. On shore, their parents began to worry and alerted the Coast Guard of their sons' adventure.

The thunder cracked, and the waves bounced, bobbing the boys' boat up and down. They saw the Coast Guard flying up ahead and seeming to stop over them. They waved up at them to let them know they were okay. They kept their eyes toward the shoreline, focused and concentrated on making it back. Hours later, they made it back to the Yacht Club, where anxious parents gave them relieved hugs. The boys and the boat were both unharmed by the tropical storm.

Not only does this story illustrate the drastic difference in our parenting today and a generation before us (I would never let Josie Lou sail out on the open ocean by herself at ten years old), but it also teaches us a great lesson in control. On the first expedition to Cat Island, the young boy thought he had it all together; he thought he knew his own boundaries and limits. It worked out okay for him on that first trip. He pushed the boundaries, and he turned out fine. He also turned out fine on the second trip, but it was a much closer call.

In this story, the tropical storm was out of the brothers' control; their obedience was in their control. In life, there are many things we cannot control, but we can always control our obedience. We often focus on trying to control the things we can't because living in obedience isn't easy. We can quickly fall out of obedience.

The beauty of this story is that even when the brothers disobeyed their parents and pushed their boundaries, their parents didn't stop loving them. They sent out the Coast Guard to find them, and the Coast Guard helped point the boys back to shore. The same is true for us: Even when we disobey God, He never stops loving us and will always rescue us. The freedom of knowing we are loved despite our past mistakes gives us joy.

God is slowly teaching me to release the desire to control every small area of my life. Holding on to control only gives us a false sense of security, leaving us empty and hollow. Our tight grip on control often causes joy to slip right through our fingertips. We can be of good cheer when we release control.

 Cheer Practice

5—Breath Prayers

Pray this scripture on an inhale and exhale.

- Inhale: one, two, three, four
- Exhale: five, six, seven, eight

Try breathing and meditating on the words or saying the words aloud on those counts.

- Inhale: For the love of Christ
- Exhale: controls us
  (2 Cor. 5:14)

- Inhale: All things work for the good
- Exhale: of those who love God
  (Rom. 8:28)

6—Scripture Callout

Let's memorize this scripture together.

Our sixth callout:

"For I know the plans I have for you," declares the Lord, "plans to prosper you and not to harm you, plans to give you hope and a future." (Jer. 29:11, NIV)

Practice saying this verse out loud, repeat it, write it down and put it somewhere that you can see it.

7—Gratitude Challenge

I believe that gratitude is the best prescription for cheerfulness. When we think about the things we are grateful for, it is hard to stay focused on our challenging circumstances. Thankfulness is not always something that comes natural to us. We have to practice.

I encourage you to write down three things that you are grateful for today. This could be in relation to what we've studied in this chapter or just related to something in your life right now. I encourage you to think of something different from the last chapter.

Thank you, Jesus, for:

_____

_____

_____

8—Spread Some Cheer

A simple way to choose cheer in our lives is to share cheer with others.

TODAY'S CHEER CHALLENGE:
WHAT'S ONE THING YOU CAN
RELEASE CONTROL OF TODAY
THAT IS AFFECTING SOMEONE ELSE?

Throughout this chapter, we discussed control and how when we hold on to control, we really are holding on to a false sense of security. Is there an area in your life you are holding on to control that is affecting someone around you? Considering the workplace, if you are in a position of leadership, you may need to release control to those you are leading to truly see them spread their wings and reach their potential. If you are in a position of being led in this season, perhaps you need to release control to your superiors, trusting in their leadership and that they are seeing the bigger picture. If your work is in your home, this might look like releasing control of a clean and ordered house and allowing your kids the space for play and creativity. This can sometimes be very challenging, but as we increase our trust in God over the details of our lives, our cheer will also increase.

PART THREE

How Do We Choose Cheer?

SEVEN

Holy Spirit

I grew up in a big family. When I say big, I mean *big*. I have twenty-one first cousins, each with around three kids each. So, you can imagine how lively our family gatherings can be. I recall one particular instance when I approached a family event and heard a voice yelling, "I need some help!" "Hey, I need some help!" As we drew closer, we discovered that the voice was coming from the swing set. "Up here! I need some help!" Following the voice, we found my little cousin perched at the top of the slide, eyes wide like saucers, looking petrified. The slide had looked fun from down below, but once he reached the top, he was scared to death. How was he going to get down? Overtaken by fear, he quickly realized that if he was going to get down, he needed some help.

When it comes to maintaining cheerfulness and experiencing the fullness of joy, we must acknowledge that we, too, are in need of assistance. Life can be challenging. Fear and anxiety can overwhelm us and rob us of our joy. In those seasons of challenge, we must remember that we do not walk alone. There's no need to push through or tough it out on our own when we're struggling. True joy is not something we can muster on our own but comes from the Spirit within us. When you need help getting your feet on solid ground, you have a Helper.

As discussed in chapter 2, the theme verse for Choosing Cheer (John 16:33) is found in the middle of what scholars call the farewell discourse—the portion of John's narrative in which Jesus prepares His disciples for his departure. Until this point, much of Jesus's teaching was in parables, but as His time on earth drew to a close, He began to speak plainly to His followers. He would be going away, but He would not leave them orphaned. He would send a Helper—the Holy Spirit.

THE HOLY SPIRIT

What comes to your mind when you hear the "Holy Spirit"? Your answer probably depends on your upbringing. If you grew up in church, chances are that your understanding of the Holy Spirit is rooted in how your church talked about, preached on, and interacted with the Holy Spirit. If you did not grow up in church, talk of the Holy Spirit may seem strange, but I hope you'll keep an open mind.

Every year at our church's Fall Jam event, we participate in Trunk-or-Treat. As we move from trunk to trunk with my daughter collecting candy, we receive all types of treats. Many people buy fun-size candy bars. You know what I'm talking about—those small Snickers, Hershey's, Twix, or Milky Way bars that give you just the tiniest taste so that you want the whole candy bar, but you know you can't have it because the small amount you had is gone and there are no full-sized candy bars in sight.

People often think about the Holy Spirit as a "fun-size" portion of God, as if He is "kind of" God or "part of" God, but not equal to God the Father and God the Son. The Spirit is the third person of the Trinity, proceeding from the Father through the Son (Ayars 2023). The Holy Spirit isn't part of God or some of God. The Holy Spirit is all of God. In addition, the Holy Spirit is a person, not an it. And we have access to the full presence and power of God through the Holy Spirit.

The problem with viewing the Spirit as a portion of God is the same as with the fun-sized candy bar. It leaves us with a taste of the Spirit, and it is sweet, but we aren't satisfied. Many of us don't know where to find the full-size or JUMBO-size version. I think that is why we often only experience part or pieces of the joy of Jesus. Because joy is a fruit of the Spirit, if we only experience part of the Spirit, we can only experience part of His joy.

Others may have a different view of the Holy Spirit. Where some people underemphasize the Spirit, there are also traditions of faith that overemphasize the Holy Spirit. Some people may not feel like they have experienced the Spirit because they haven't experienced Him in a certain way. The Holy Spirit is a living person, not an experience or feeling to be conjured up.

That's not to say we won't have tangible experiences with the Spirit. I have certainly experienced the power of the Spirit in my life, but I most often experience Him in the sweet and quiet moments such as when just the right scripture is whispered to my heart, almost audibly, or when I sit up out of a dead sleep in the middle of the night with goose bumps on my arm and a burning desire to pray for someone, only later to discover they had a need at that same moment, or the nudge to "talk to that person" in the cafe or to pick up the phone and call someone. I have experienced the supernatural strength to get through the day when I don't feel like I can make it another step. I have experienced supernatural healing in a quiet way. The Spirit's role isn't always dramatic and huge; it is often small, sweet, and quiet and certainly cannot be manipulated. The Spirit is God's presence with us, helping us and nudging us along to a life closer to God, revealing to us what in our life is distracting us from God or what sin is separating us from God.

One of my favorite Bible teachers, Tara-Leigh Cobble, often reminds her students, "Don't scream where scripture whispers." When discussing the Holy Spirit, this is important—we must look at what scripture says about the Spirit. Paul writes about the gifts of the Spirit in 1 Corinthians 12, "There are different kinds of spiritual gifts, but the same Spirit is the source of them all" (v. 4, NLT). He writes that the purpose of all gifts is to help one another. Paul lists the gifts of the Spirit: wise counsel, special knowledge, faith, healing, miracles, prophecy, discernment, the ability to speak in unknown languages, and the ability to interpret the languages (1 Cor. 12: 8–10). He concludes, "It is the one and only Spirit who distributes all these gifts. He alone decides which gift each person should have" (v. 11, NLT). We would need a whole book to begin understanding the gifts of the Spirit, but we mention them here briefly to aid in our study.

While reading what the entire scriptures say about the Spirit is essential, if we look specifically at what Jesus teaches about the Holy Spirit, we have the best idea of how to expect Him to move and work in our lives. Right before our key verse in John 16, Jesus tells His disciples, "It is to your advantage that I go away, for if I do not go away, the Helper will not come to you" (v. 7). Can you imagine hearing this as a disciple? Your rabbi, your teacher that you've given up your life to follow, tells you that He will leave you and that it will be better for you. I imagine the doubts that filled their minds. Although they would have been familiar with how the Spirit rested on religious leaders, kings, prophets, and judges in the Hebrew Scriptures, and while they would have known stories of how the Spirit rested on and empowered people chosen by God for a season or task, they still had a minimal understanding of the Holy Spirit at this point. They would've understood the Spirit as coming and resting on important people chosen by God in His story.

Jesus continues to explain, "And when He [the Helper] has come, He will convict the world of sin, and of righteousness, and of judgment" (John 16:8, NKJV). In this description, Jesus gives us an outline of some of the roles or functions of the Spirit for His followers. Let's look a little deeper into each of these.

HELPER

First, Jesus calls the Spirit our *Helper*. (I could testify a million times to the Spirit's role of helper in my own life, but we'll stick to what Jesus describes here.) Next, Jesus explains *how* the Holy Spirit will help us: The Spirit will convict the world of sin. Conviction is one of the greatest gifts of the Spirit, one of the biggest ways He acts as our Helper. When the Spirit convicts us, He reveals the areas where we are not yielded to Him. He shows us what areas we are holding on to control or seeking our own ways of doing things. One simple example of this in my life is my tongue. So often, I want to think that I speak to others in a way that honors Jesus, but the Spirit often convicts me when I respond in anger and defensiveness, instead of with patience and grace. It's easier for me to submit to Him in the big decisions, where I feel helpless, but to submit to Him and yield to Him in the way I treat people in my daily interactions is a little bit more difficult.

Most of us don't like conviction and it can be hard for us to see it as helpful. Time and time again, I can point to the gift of the conviction of the Spirit in my life. He protects me and gives me a warning sign—a sense in my gut that I'm headed in a direction that is not best for me. Being open and responsive for the conviction of the Spirit allows us to receive the full blessing of His role as our Helper.

If we back up a few chapters before, in John 14, we read, "But the Helper, the Holy Spirit, whom the Father will send in My name, He will teach you all things, and bring to your remembrance all that I have said to you" (v. 26, NKJV). This description of the Holy Spirit from Jesus gives us two key ways the Holy Spirit acts as helper in our lives: (1) He *teaches* us. (2) He *reminds* us.

One of the biggest ways I experience the Holy Spirit as my helper is when I am studying the scriptures. He teaches me through his Word. I can sense Him giving me understanding or prompting me to look closer or further into a verse. He continually shows me new insights in the scriptures.

The word of God is living and active; the Spirit breathes life into the scriptures, and the words affect our very hearts. Have you ever prayed and felt a scripture whisper across your heart in response? Maybe it was a scripture you'd recently read or one you stored in your heart long ago. The Holy Spirit not only teaches us the scriptures but also reminds us of them right when we need them.

A distinction that I think is important for us to make when looking at this role of the Holy Spirit is that Jesus says He will help us bring to remembrance. The Spirit helps us remember. This is why we've put such an emphasis on memorizing scripture in our Cheer Practice sections. The Spirit brings to mind the words of God that we have stored in our hearts. He can't help us remember things that aren't there. This is how we cooperate and walk in step with the Spirit. The Spirit is at work in our lives, but we have a part to play. The Holy Spirit is our *Helper,* not our *Do-er.* When we cooperate with Him, yield to Him, and depend on Him, we experience His power. If we kick our feet up on the couch or put our head in the sand, we miss out on the work that He is doing in and around us.

Just a few verses earlier in John 14:16, Jesus tells His disciples, "And I will ask the Father, and he will give you another Helper, to be with you forever . . . the Spirit of Truth." The Greek word for Helper as it is used here is parakleitos and is described as, "an intercessor, consoler, comforter, advocate, helper." The comforter portion is specifically described as "to comfort, encourage, or one called upon to help" (Baker 2013 p.2232). Jesus told His disciples and He is telling us, another way the Holy Spirit helps us is to comfort us. And according to Psalm 94, our comfort has a direct correlation with our cheer:

> When doubts filled my mind, your comfort gave me renewed hope and cheer. (Ps. 94:19, NLT)

The Holy Spirit will comfort us and restore our joy. When we reflect on the "Four C's That Cheat Us of Cheerfulness," we can notice the Spirit works as Helper in these roles. Regardless of the challenges we might be facing, the Spirit reminds us that God has been faithful before and that He will be faithful again. In our connections, the Spirit helps us to show love and joy to those we care about. The Spirit allows us to extend a supernatural forgiveness to those who have wronged us. The Spirit guards our hearts from comparison, helping us to find our contentment in God. The Spirit helps us to loosen our tight grip of control, trusting that He is guiding us and helping us along the way. The more we understand the Holy Spirit's role as Helper, the more we will be able to restore cheer in these areas.

CONVINCER

Jesus also says that the Spirit convinces the world of righteousness and judgment (John 16:8). Not only is the Holy Spirit going to convict people of their sin, He will help them know the righteousness we have in Jesus and how to come out of sin and into life with God. "Righteousness" and "judgment" can be intimidating at first glance. We can hear these words and immediately feel defeated. Jesus changed the way that we think about these words. He redeemed these two words to become hopeful words for His followers.

Paul helps us here: "For our sake he made him to be sin who knew no sin, so that in him we might become the righteousness of God" (2 Cor. 5:21).

Because of the work of Jesus on the cross and His resurrection from the grave, we have the righteousness of Christ. Righteousness means right standing with God. It is not something we can earn for ourselves; it is something only God can do on our behalf.

We have been "covered . . . with the robe of righteousness" (Isa. 61:10). When God looks at us, He sees the righteousness of Jesus, not all of our sins. This gives us great hope. We no longer have to fear judgment. Now, this doesn't mean we should do what we want. When we live in the Spirit and seek to honor God with our lives, we don't have to live afraid. We live with a healthy respect and a great desire to be obedient, but we know we can't measure up; we can't do it by ourselves. We need God's spirit to work on our behalf.

Romans 3:23 reminds us that we "have all sinned and fall short of the glory of God." The Spirit convinces us that our righteousness is secured in Jesus's death on the cross and resurrection from the grave. He convinces us that when we face the judgment because of our sin, we will be counted righteous because of Christ. Knowing, or being convinced of judgment, encourages us to respond to our convictions and allows us to live in the freedom of Christ. We are completely dependent on Him. We cannot enter eternity, life forever with God, without Him. It is so easy for us to live our lives from a place of self-dependence, thinking we can do it all on our own. It is the American way. But the truth is, we desperately need the Spirit's help. The quicker we come to this realization, the quicker the Spirit can remove pride from our heart and lead us down a path that honors God.

GUIDE TO TRUTH

Finally, Jesus says that the Spirit will "guide you into all truth" and "take what is mine and declare it to you" (John 16:13–15). One of the Spirit's main roles is to help us to understand what truth is. He is our compass, directing us to what is true in Christ and what is not. The quest for truth has plagued human beings since the beginning of time. Philosophers, scientists, and thinkers have answered the question of "what is truth?" many, many different ways.

Jesus shows up on the scene and begins to teach something different about truth. He says, "I am the way, and the truth, and the life" (John 14:6). This would have really shaken up the current societal beliefs about truth. One person is the truth? That would've been unthinkable. In the same conversation we find the verse, "[I] will give you another Helper," and He goes on to describe the helper as "the Spirit of truth" (John 14:16–17). Jesus sets a new standard for truth, and He promises His disciples that the Helper, the Holy Spirit, will guide them into that truth. Earlier in his ministry, Jesus said to the Jews who had believed in Him, "If you abide in my word, you are truly my disciples, and you will know the truth, and the truth will set you free" (John 8:31–32).

The truth will set us free. That is why we search for it and long for it. We desire freedom—freedom from the things that enslave us or hold us captive, freedom from our own thoughts, and freedom from pleasing others. The list could go on and on. The Gospel writer, John, is making it clear that Jesus is the way to truth and that through that truth, we find and experience true freedom. Based on Jesus's teaching, he argues that both of these things—truth and freedom—are only made possible by the power of the Holy Spirit working in us. Paul affirms this in his second letter to the church in Corinth when he writes, "Now the Lord is the Spirit, and where the Spirit of the Lord is, there is freedom" (2 Cor. 3:17).

When I think about freedom in Christ, I think about one of my favorite books, *The Chronicles of Narnia* by C. S. Lewis. I read the series as a child and was captivated by the story and the characters. I read them again as an adult and was enchanted by the scriptural references and spiritual significance to the story. A beautiful scene at the end of the last novel is where the characters are all entering a new land. They each are in awe of the beauty around them, and they are struggling to describe what they are seeing—how this new land is like the old one but it is even better. Lewis writes, "

The difference between the old Narnia and the new Narnia was like that. The new one was a deeper country: every rock and flower and blade of grass looked as if it meant more."

Everything was richer. The same, but different. More beautiful, more wonderful, restored. As the scene continues:

It was the Unicorn who summed up what everyone was feeling. He stamped his right fore-hoof on the ground and neighed, and then cried, "I have come home at last! This is my real country! I belong here. This is the land I've been looking for all of my life, though I never knew it till now. The reason why we loved the old Narnia is that it sometimes looked a little like this. Bree-hee-hee! Come further up, come further in!" (Lewis 2005, p. 195–197)

All the characters agree, and as the Unicorn takes off in a full gallop, the most amazing thing happens. The humans and other creatures can keep up with him. They race through the land, wind whipping around them. They ran faster and faster, "but no one got tired or out of breath." (p. 197).

As I was thinking about the freedom we have in Jesus, this scene came to mind. It is such a powerful picture of heaven. And just as in this story the Old Narnia looked like the real and true forever Narnia, it is the same with Earth. As Jesus prayed to the Father, "Your kingdom come, your will be done, on earth as it is in heaven" (Matt. 6:9). Every day we are on Earth, the Father is beckoning us, "Come further up and further in." Into more of His presence, more of His joy, more of His freedom. I want to take off running, faster and faster, closer and closer to Jesus.

The disciples would not yet have had a reference point for the indwelling of the Spirit as we understand it today. God—not "fun-sized" but all of God—is ever-present with us. When we understand this, we understand why Jesus was able to confidently say, "It will be better for you if I go away."

As modern-day Jesus followers, we have something that the disciples didn't yet have. This is hard to imagine because I can't think of anything better than Jesus in bodily form right next to me. It's almost as if He says to them, *Now you have me walking beside you, but then you will have me inside you. My very presence will be in you. He will be able to help you in ways that even I can't.*

When Jesus gave himself up for us, the veil of the temple was torn from top to bottom, and this signified that God's presence has been made available to all of us. We now have access to the presence of God, so when we believe in Jesus and when we submit our lives to him and ask Him to come to us and dwell with us, the Holy Spirit takes up residence inside our very being. What a gift! When we begin to understand this and how it affects us, we begin to unlock the key to more cheerfulness and joy in our lives despite our circumstances. I want to go "further up and further in."

JOY-GIVER

In John 15 we read Jesus's words, "I am the vine, you are the branches. Whoever abides in me and I in him, bears much fruit, for apart from me, you can do nothing" (v. 5).

This notion of fruit-bearing comes from Jesus, and it is wrapped up in his conversation and teachings on the Holy Spirit. It gives us a good lens through which to look at Paul's words in Galatians 5: "But the fruit of the Spirit is love, joy, peace, patience, kindness, goodness, faithfulness, gentleness, self-control; against such things there is no law" (vv. 22–23).

Paul outlines for us what life in the Spirit should look like. It should be evident on the outside, through our words and actions, that we abide with Jesus and his Spirit.

Many of us grew up learning about the fruit of the Spirit in Sunday school. Maybe you learned the song, or maybe you had a coloring sheet. We currently have a puzzle for my little girl with the fruit of the Spirit. My friend Kim dressed up as the fruit of the Spirit one year for our church's fall festival. It can be something that we think of as cute and good, but we can often breeze over the significance of this passage. In John 15, Jesus tells His disciples that the Father is the vinedresser and that He removes the branches that do not bear fruit. When I look at my life, I want to see fruit.

My former pastor preached a sermon one Sunday that I will never forget. He spoke on the fruit of the Spirit and I thought, "Oh good, another sermon on the fruit of the Spirit," but as he started, he said something that caught my undivided attention. He asked the congregation if we had ever noticed that "fruit" is singular. He continued that many people mistakenly use the plural "fruits" when talking about this passage. He argued that the singularity of the fruit was a very important detail in the scripture, not to be overlooked. His point was that we can't pick and choose our fruit. We can't bear peace without patience or gentleness without self-control. When we are living life in step with the Spirit, we bear His fruit. All of it works together to show the world who God is.

This was a huge revelation to me. The Spirit used this teaching to convict me and point me to His righteousness. Joy is something that comes pretty natural to me, but patience . . . not so much. It was a reality check for me and became a catalyst for me to seek more of the Spirit in my life.

As we have an increase of the Spirit in our lives, we will experience an increase in fruit. And I want that. I began to pray daily, "Empty me of myself and fill me with your Spirit that I might bear your fruit." I am convinced that this is a prayer God delights in answering. While the fruit is singular, I want to zoom in and take a closer look at JOY in the Spirit. In a book where we've discussed cheer/joy, it is so incredibly important for us to know that the Holy Spirit is the *joy-giver*.

As He continues in His farewell discourse, right after He talks about these roles of the Holy Spirit, Jesus says to His disciples, "You will be sorrowful, but your sorrow will turn into joy" (John 16:20). He is predicting His upcoming death and resurrection, but the disciples don't yet understand that. He goes on to say, "Your hearts will rejoice, and no one will take your joy from you" (John 16:22).

In the following chapter, when Jesus is praying to his Father on behalf of His current followers and the followers to come (you and me), He prays, "That they may have my joy fulfilled in themselves" (John 17:13). Jesus desires for us to have His joy. He longs for us to experience His joy while we are on this side of heaven. He makes it clear that the Holy Spirit will be our Helper, our key to experiencing this joy He is describing. True joy cannot be found apart from him.

If we believe that the Holy Spirit is *all* of God, then we believe that the very power of God that raised Jesus up from the grave is living inside me and inside you. We also believe living in the Spirit is key to living a cheerful life. The Holy Spirit takes over our conscience and works to lead us to where we should go and away from where we shouldn't. The Holy Spirit works in us to help us understand the scripture when we read it. And He draws scripture to our mind when we need to remember it. The Holy Spirit is how we are able to have cheer or joy in the midst of impossible circumstances.

When we feel like we've hit a wall, the Holy Spirit reminds us of all the ways that God has been faithful in the past and that allows us to have hope in the present. He gives us a supernatural ability to have joy even in hard things. But when we neglect the Spirit, when we aren't open to his leading, we find ourselves without hope and without cheer.

Romans 8 tells us:

> For those who live according to the flesh set their minds on the things of the flesh, but those who live according to the Spirit set their minds on the things of the Spirit. For to set the mind on the flesh is death, but to set the mind on the Spirit is life and peace. (vv. 5–6)

I don't know about you, but I want to feel life and peace. Today, how are we setting our mind on the spirit? Scripture tells us that "the joy of the Lord is our strength" (Neh. 8:10). **If we miss out on the Spirit, we miss out on the joy. If we miss out on the joy, we miss out on the strength.** When we stand peering down a slide that is a little taller than it looked from the ground, let's not be afraid to call for help. And may we rest in trusting assurance that our Helper is here.

 # Cheer Practice

5—*Breath Prayers*

Pray this scripture on an inhale and exhale.

- Inhale: one, two, three, four
- Exhale: five, six, seven, eight

Try breathing and meditating on the words or saying the words aloud on those counts.

- Inhale: Live by the Spirit
- Exhale: Keep in step with the Spirit
  (Gal. 5:25)

- Inhale: Where the Spirit of the Lord is
- Exhale: there is freedom
  (2 Cor. 3:17)

6—*Scripture Callout*

Let's memorize this scripture together.
Our seventh callout:

If the Spirit of him who raised Jesus from the dead dwells in you, he who raised Christ Jesus from the dead will also give life to your mortal bodies through his Spirit who dwells in you. (Rom. 8:11)

Practice saying this verse out loud, repeat it, write it down, and put it somewhere that you can see it.

7—Gratitude Challenge

I believe that gratitude is the best prescription for cheerfulness. When we think about the things we are grateful for, it is hard to stay focused on our challenging circumstances. Thankfulness is not always something that comes natural to us. We have to practice.

I encourage you to write down three things that you are grateful for today. This could be in relation to what we've studied in this chapter or just related to something in your life right now. I encourage you to think of something different from the last chapter.

Thank you, Jesus, for:

_____

_____

_____

8—Spread Some Cheer

A simple way to choose cheer in our lives is to share cheer with others.

TODAY'S CHEER CHALLENGE:
ASK THE SPIRIT TO LEAD YOU IN HOW
TO SHARE CHEER WITH SOMEONE TODAY.

In this chapter, we discussed the role of the Holy Spirit. Spend some time seeking Him and listening to where He is leading you. One example I think of is the "Monday Night Dinners" that were shared at my mother-in-law's house. While Preston and I were dating in college, I was included in a fun tradition his mom had begun. Preston's family home was near our university. His mom cooked dinner every Monday night, and our job was to fill her big dining room table. We never knew how many people would show up, and usually, we had to drag more chairs around the table to make room for everyone. She provided the space and the hospitality; Preston and his brother invited the guests. It was like a revolving door, different people every week. Often, Preston would invite someone who was typically excluded or was down on their luck. There are so many ways to spread cheer. Preston's family leveraged their resources to bless college students. Don't overcomplicate it! Ask the Spirit to show you how to spread cheer this week.

EIGHT

Prayer

W e would be remiss to discuss Jesus's joy without discussing prayer. While we touched on prayer in chapter 6, where we discussed waiting and releasing control to God, there is more to delve into about the importance of prayer in choosing cheer. Joy and prayer are interconnected, and we see this lived out in Jesus's ministry. Over and over again, He met with the Father in prayer.

As I mentioned earlier, Jesus's death on the cross and resurrection from the grave are the ultimate examples of joy amid sorrow. Joy had to be present even in the pain of the cross because joy is a part of Jesus's nature and character and couldn't be stripped from Him in these moments of intense difficulty. Anticipating the moments ahead of Him, Jesus met the Father in prayer as His first priority.

We often use the Lord's Prayer as our guide for how to pray, and this prayer has helped me immensely over the years. Another prayer of Jesus that helps teach us about how to pray is what is known as the "high priestly prayer." This prayer is at the end of His farewell discourse and recorded in John 17. It is Jesus's wrap-up and His final remarks. It immediately follows the theme verse for our book. Jesus says, "In the world you will have tribulation; but be of good cheer, I have overcome the world" (John 16:33). Then the scripture reads, "When Jesus had spoken these words, he lifted up his eyes to heaven and said, 'Father, the hour has come; glorify your Son that the Son may glorify you'" (John 17:1). Then e launches into an absolutely beautiful prayer, taking up all of John 17.

This prayer gives us a precious glimpse into the heart and mind of Jesus. It shows us Jesus's priorities and concerns for the world, His followers, and those coming after them. Jesus shows us how to bring these concerns before the Father. In this prayer, we can break down Jesus's conversation with God to help us have a model for our own prayers. Here, we see Jesus teach us that we can (1) bring our own requests to the Father; (2) pray for others, our friends, and our families; (3) pray for those in our lives who need to come to know Jesus; (4) ask for unity. By following Jesus's example in prayer, we allow ourselves to cultivate a deeper relationship with Him, resulting in deeper joy.

BRING YOUR REQUESTS

Jesus begins His prayer by conversing with the Father about the imminent events ahead of him. He knew what was coming, and He took it to God in prayer. He gives us a model of what it looks like to bring our troubles and concerns before God. Nothing is too big or too small to bring to the Father.

Meeting with the Father in prayer, I have experienced great joy. Spending time with Him is my soul's delight. Some of the most joyous moments I remember are found in moments of prayer. This could be when staring at the ocean, being reminded of the vastness of God while the breeze hits my face and runs through my hair, reminding me of his nearness. Or on a walk in the woods or a park, looking at the height of the trees and hearing the sweet songs of the birds. A whispered prayer of thanks for my daughter's little giggle and the light in her eyes. I often experience joy sitting on the little corner of our fluffy white couch in our living room, with coffee in hand and a Bible and prayer journal spread across my lap before sunrise. In closeness with God and communion with God, we experience true joy.

PRAYING FOR OTHERS

As Jesus prays for the disciples and those who will come to believe in Him (you and me), He says, "I told them many things while I was with them in this world so they would be filled with my joy" (John 17:13, NLT). By this statement, Jesus reveals that the purpose or end result of what He said to the disciples was their joy. All of His teachings in the farewell discourse and all of His statements in this prayer culminate in joy. However, when we read what He prays, this can be hard for us to grasp.

Jesus prays to the Father, "I have given them your word, and the world has hated them because they are not of the world, just as I am not of the world" (John 17:14). Jesus reiterates that life as one of His followers is not easy or trouble-free. He acknowledges that they will be hated by others and also acknowledges that He knows what that feels like.

Then He prays something hard for us to read, "I do not ask that you take them out of the world, but that you guard them from the evil one" (John 17:15). My initial question is—why? Why not take us out of the world if it is hard and if where you are going is better? Jesus always displays great intentionality behind what He says and does. There is meaning behind this statement: Any suffering we face will result in our good and His glory (Rom. 8:28). This part of the prayer echoes our theme verse, John 16:33. In His prayer to His Father, Jesus restates that trouble is a guarantee for His followers.

Reflecting on how Jesus prays on behalf of His disciples in their collective time of trouble, I think about how Preston has done this for me in our marriage. Analogies of our human experience fall short when attempting to demonstrate the things of God. Still, we will use a human analogy because it is what we have available. Preston often prays for me when I don't know what to pray for myself. If I am particularly stressed, worn down, exhausted, or sick, he will often sense that in me, and before we retire for the night, he will kneel down next to our bed, reach over and take hold of my hand, and pray the words that I don't have at that moment.

I remember one particular night when I had allowed my worries from the day to get the best of me. I responded to Preston with a short temper, and he reached over, grabbed my hand, and said, "Can I pray for you?" My answer came as quick and as fast as my anger, "No, thank you." I took my hand back and turned the other way. A few minutes later, I looked at him, reached for his hand, and said, "Please pray for me."

At the moment of his original invitation, I was not responding in the ways of the Spirit. I gave in to worry and fear and resisted God's gentle nudging through my husband. I didn't want to talk to God at that moment because I knew I wasn't obeying him, I wasn't acting like Him, and I wasn't living out love. We often resist God when we know we aren't living like him, but these are the precise moments when we must come to Him. When I took a minute to think about it, I knew prayer was exactly what I needed. I also knew that allowing Preston to pray over me the words I couldn't pray for myself was the best thing I could do then. As he prayed, I nodded in agreement as tears rolled down my cheeks. I was assured of God's love for me and His desire to draw me back to Himself. I recall other instances where the reverse has been true—when Preston experienced something particularly difficult, and I have had the privilege of praying over him.

Jesus modeled this for His disciples. Imagine how they would have felt after hearing all that Jesus had said to them up until this point in the farewell discourse. They would have been unsettled, confused, and most likely afraid. Jesus could sense this in His closest friends. So, He stopped and prayed for them.

Prayer is a personal practice, and it is also a communal practice. We are to pray for one another. In life's difficult moments, do we have the courage to offer prayer to those around us? In my experience, I have found that people rarely refuse prayer. Even if they don't have an active relationship with God or if they practice another religion, people don't usually turn down an offer to pray. In the South, we habitually say, "Aww, I'll pray for you." Unfortunately, this statement is often equivalent to "Bless your heart." It is something that is said because it is what good Christians say, and then most people move on. I wonder how many times people actually pray for what they say they will pray for. I wonder what change we would see if we truly began to pray for those around us.

May we be genuine and bold in offering prayer to those around us. Recently, a friend I hadn't seen in a while shared a particularly difficult situation they were walking through. I listened intently, and when they wrapped up, I resisted the desire to offer them my feedback or commentary, sensing from the Spirit that they didn't need that; they needed prayer. So, I took a deep breath and asked, "Can I pray for you?" We bowed our heads in the middle of a parking lot on a hot summer day in Mississippi, and I offered a simple prayer for the Lord to meet them in their time of trouble and give them the wisdom and peace to walk through it. I asked that God's presence would surround them. I didn't say anything profound or significant, but their damp eyes told me that the Spirit's leading is always the best thing to follow.

PRAYING FOR THOSE TO COME

Jesus prayed, "I do not ask for these only, but also those who will believe in me through their word" (John 17:20). This prayer was for you and me and for all who would come to know Jesus after He spoke it to the Father. In studying this passage, I was personally convicted at how little I pray in this way.

Some of our dear friends live this out beautifully. Johnny grew up in a non-Christian home and came to know Jesus when he was in high school. A friend at school discipled him, read scripture with him, and took him to meet with his pastor when they encountered questions they didn't understand. After many years and lots of questions, Johnny gave his life to Jesus and was baptized. This was a big deal to his family, and his mother was initially very disappointed in him and was not accepting of his new Christian beliefs. This was very challenging for him because he and his mother were very close. He prayed for his mother and for their relationship to be restored. Over the years, his mother has accepted his beliefs while she continues to practice her religion. They have found common ground in their love for one another, but Johnny longs for his mother to experience the joy and peace he has found in his relationship with Jesus.

Johnny and his wife live their whole lives on a mission to introduce others to Jesus. They both are in nonministerial jobs but live in a way that brings others in. They invite people into their home and to become a part of their family. They pray for their friends and family members who do not know Jesus and ask other trusted believers to do the same. Almost every time I talk to them, they tell me about a new friend they had over for dinner and ask me to pray for them to be open to hearing and receiving the gospel.

These friends are not pushy. Instead, they are welcoming and inviting. Everyone loves them and wants to be around them. They are a beautiful example of caring for and praying for people like Jesus did.

How can we pray for those who need to know Jesus? Perhaps you are longing for an adult child to return to their faith, praying for another precious family member or friend to come to know Jesus for the first time, or praying for someone who hurt or wronged you. Know that as much as you have prayed for them, Jesus prayed for them too. The scripture tells us that He actively intercedes on our behalf to the Father. We can rest assured that as our hearts long for our loved ones to know Him, His heart's desire is the same.

ASK FOR UNITY

One of the significant themes in Jesus's prayer in John 17 is unity. In verse 11, Jesus prayed, "Keep them in your name, which you have given me, that they may be one, even as we are one." Later in verse 21, He prayed, "that they may all be one, just as you,

Father, are in me, and I in you, that they also may be in us." Jesus prays for His followers to be united. Perhaps He anticipates this will be a problem for us, so He spends a large portion of the prayer focused on praying for unity.

One of my former pastors always taught us to look at the "so that's" in scripture. This passage has a big "so that." Immediately following asking the Father for unity, Jesus prays, "So that the world may believe that you have sent me" (John 17:21). He repeats it again a few verses later, showing us its importance.

When we look at the church's state today, we see many arguments and disagreements. This was never Jesus's design. If our unity is how people will know Jesus is the one true God, how will our disunity prohibit people from coming to know him? Let's be committed to praying as Jesus did for unity among believers. Let's allow Him to bring unity to others through us.

We often overlook the simple act of praying for joy. What would it look like for us to experience more of Jesus's joy? When we feel like we are just going through the motions, we can pray, "Lord, help me to find joy in what I'm doing." When we are in a pit of sorrow, we can ask, "God, help me to see your light here." Simple prayers of dependence help transform our attitude and mindset.

JOY, GLORY, AND SUFFERING

As Jesus was wrapping up, He prayed:

> The glory that you have given me I have given to them, that
> they may be one even as we are one, I in them and you in
> me, that they may become perfectly one, so that the world
> may know that you sent me and loved them even as you loved
> me. Father, I desire that they also, whom you have given me,
> may be with me where I am, to see my glory that you have
> given me because you loved me before the foundation of the
> world. (John 17:22–24)

Leading up to this section, He has prayed and acknowledged that we will share in His suffering and the hate the world has for Him. Now, He prays that the Father would allow us to share in His glory. He says to the Father, "The glory that you have given me I have given to them" (John 17:22). Paul explains this in Romans 8:17 (NLT), "And since we are his children, we are his heirs. In fact, together with Christ, we are heirs of God's glory. But if we are to share his glory, we must also share his suffering."

We can't have one without the other. We desire to share in the glory but don't want to share in the suffering. As William Barclay writes in his commentary on John 17, "Jesus did not pray that his disciples should be taken out of this world. He never prayed that they might find escape; he prayed that they might find victory" (Barclay 2017, p. 250–251).

As we already discussed in chapter 2, suffering and joy are also interconnected. Hebrews 12:2 tells us, "For the joy set before him he endured the cross." Romans 5:3 says we are to "rejoice in our sufferings." First Peter 4: 12–13 (NLT) says, "Dear friends, don't be surprised at the fiery trials you are going through, as if something strange were happening to you. Instead, be very glad— for these trials make you partners with Christ in his suffering, so that you will have the wonderful joy of seeing his glory when it is revealed to all the world." Here, we see the connectedness of joy, glory, and suffering.

What does sharing in his suffering look like for us? Most of us aren't actively being persecuted for our faith in Jesus the way that some of our brothers and sisters are around the world. We can feel that we aren't suffering. But let's look at these verses in context with what Jesus says in the rest of the farewell discourse, especially in chapter 16. As Jesus refers to it here, we can conclude that suffering is more than persecution. Suffering could appear as a shocking and hopeless diagnosis, ridicule or exclusion, a temptation, or a difficult circumstance. Unfortunately, Jesus promises us that we will suffer as His followers. Still, thankfully, as a result of or a reward for suffering, He also promises us joy in this life and glory in the next.

My husband, Preston, tells a story about John 17. Every time this passage comes up in a sermon or something we read, he mentions a specific experience that left a mark on him. In high school, he visited New Orleans for a national leadership conference at Tulane University. He attended leadership sem- inars throughout the day, and at night, in the dorm room, he would read through the book of John. One night, he read John 17, and one particular verse stood out to him. Jesus prayed, "I have revealed you to those whom you gave me" (v. 6, NIV). In response to this verse, Preston whispered a heartfelt prayer to God, "Reveal yourself to me, Father."

The next afternoon, a group of students from all over the country went on an outing. With the hot New Orleans pavement under their feet, the group started out to the French Market—an open-air market in the heart of the French Quarter. They walked around, exploring all of the different vendors and their items. Preston passed a table where a man sat with a genuine smile. As the group moved on, Preston felt a nudge from the Spirit to go back to that table.

He split off from the group and walked up to the man. As Preston walked closer, he realized the man was selling his poetry. My husband picked up one of the poetry books, and as he began to read, the man asked him, "Do you know Jesus?" Preston replied, "Yes, sir, I do." He grinned from ear to ear, shook his hand, and said, "Brother! Hallelujah!" In the following moments, he said "hallelujah" a few more times; Preston says he emphasized the "YAH." He then asked Preston, "Do you know what hallelujah means?" Preston replied, "Praise God." The man looked at him and said, "Be more specific." Preston looked at him with questioning eyes. He replied, "In this city, there are many gods, but we worship Yahweh."

He told Preston that to find out more about who God is, he should read John 17. Preston stared at him, mouth slack, unsure if he heard him correctly. He went on to explain why John 17 is such a significant passage. Jesus proclaimed that He came to reveal who God is. He recited the poem out of the book Preston was holding entitled, "The Strength to Face the Day." His strong voice read out beautiful stanzas describing the strength God gives us when we pray. Words of hope and reminders that God will stand with us, whether the day brings sunshine or rain.

Preston purchased the book of poems and wrapped up his conversation with the man. He couldn't believe it. He had asked God to reveal Himself, and God answered. Not in a wild or crazy way, but in an "I see you and I hear you" kind of way. He remembers walking away to find the rest of the group with joy in his step and feeling emboldened to share his faith with those he was with at the conference. He recalls feeling a deep sense of joy in that moment of obedience—feeling a nudge of the Spirit and turning around to talk to this man.

Prayer is often a last resort instead of our first option, but this is where the groundwork begins for choosing cheer. This is where all the ideas we've discussed so far come together. In prayer, we release control, fight for our relationships, unwind the tangles of comparison, and find the confidence to face our challenges. In prayer, we ask God to help us where we struggle in the "Four C's That Cheat Us of Cheerfulness" we've discussed.

As this simple yet beautiful poem reminds us, even though we are not sure if this day will hold joy or sorrow, sunshine or rain, or a mixture of it all, prayer is our access to the strength to face the day. Through prayer, we can find joy to endure the sorrow and find sunshine amid the rain.

 Cheer Practice

5—Breath Prayers

Pray this scripture on an inhale and exhale.

- Inhale: one, two, three, four
- Exhale: five, six, seven, eight

Try breathing and meditating on the words or saying the words aloud on those counts.

- Inhale: Do not be anxious
- Exhale: Instead, pray
  (Phil. 4:6)

- Inhale: O, God,
- Exhale: hear my prayer
  (Ps. 54:2)

6—Scripture Callout

Let's memorize this scripture together.
    Our eighth callout:

Rejoice always, pray without ceasing, give thanks in all circumstances; for this is the will of God in Christ Jesus for you. (1 Thess. 5:16–18)

Practice saying this verse out loud, repeat it, write it down and put it somewhere that you can see it.

7—Gratitude Challenge

I believe that gratitude is the best prescription for cheerfulness. When we think about the things we are grateful for, it is hard to stay focused on our challenging circumstances. Thankfulness is not always something that comes natural to us. We have to practice.

I encourage you to write down three things that you are grateful for today. This could be in relation to what we've studied in this chapter or just related to something in your life right now. I encourage you to think of something different from the last chapter.

Thank you, Jesus, for:

_____

_____

_____

8—*Spread Some Cheer*

TODAY'S CHEER CHALLENGE: WHO CAN YOU PRAY FOR TODAY?

In this chapter, we discussed prayer in light of Jesus's prayer in John 17. As Jesus modeled in praying for His disciples in their time of need, who can you pray for today? Praying for others is one of our highest callings as followers of Jesus and is often overlooked. Who could you send a text or give a call to today to let them know they are being held in prayer? My dear mentor and friend, Cynthia, lives this out in a beautiful way. Every time you talk to her, she asks, "How can I pray for you?" Because of her reliance and closeness to the Holy Spirit, she also intuitively can pick up on when someone might need prayer. Then, she follows up. You'll get a text the next day, a card a few days later, and a phone call a few days after that. When Cynthia says she is praying for you, you can count on it. Despite her own particularly difficult set of circumstances, Cynthia is constantly encouraging those around her. This may seem a bit intimidating, and you may think, "I'm not on that level." As we've discussed, simple steps help set priorities and make habits. Perhaps you can start by just sending a text message to someone you know is having a difficult time and let them know you are praying for them. What small step can you take today toward a life of praying for others?

NINE

Intention

Have you ever been shopping and had bad luck? You know what I'm talking about?

You go through a store, pick out your items, feel pretty good, and head to the dressing room. You think you've selected some excellent options, but then you start trying things on. Somehow, your items don't look the same as they did on the mannequin. You keep trying and trying, but nothing is working. Eventually, you leave the clothes in the dressing room, and you walk out of the store having purchased nothing, thinking you'll just come back and try another day.

Choosing Cheer can sometimes feel like this. You try on cheerfulness because it looks perfect on the hanger, but when you put it on, and you move around in it, you think, "Ugh, I don't know if this really feels right." The Bible has something to say about this in the book of Proverbs. Proverbs is a book of wisdom written by Solomon, King David's son. Solomon asked God for wisdom and became the wisest man on earth.

It would be prudent to take note of his teachings. In Proverbs 15:13, Solomon says,

> A glad heart makes a cheerful face, but by sorrow of heart, the spirit is crushed. The heart of him who has understanding seeks knowledge, but the mouth of fools feeds on folly.

The word used here for cheerful literally is translated as "better or greater." In this passage, Solomon is referencing that a glad heart or a cheerful face is better or greater than the sorrow of the heart that crushes the spirit. This might seem obvious at first look, but there is something deeper here for us to learn. Cheerful, as used in this passage, is also translated as "to adorn or to dress" (Baker 2013, p. 1725). Our glad hearts should adorn or dress our faces as cheerful. In other words, the joy we have on the inside should be apparent on the outside. Our outward expression is a direct reflection of our inward state.

As followers of Jesus, our joy should look different than the frantic pace of the world around us. This does not mean that we should put on our cheerful face when it's not genuine. Remember, we know that based on the Greek words, we can interchange the word "cheerful" with "joy." Joy is not something that you put on today and take off tomorrow. Joy is eternal; according to scripture, we know that our joy cannot be taken away from us (John 16:22) and should not change based on our circumstances. When we look in the mirror, and we find our face isn't very cheerful, we should train ourselves to take a look at our heart instead of our circumstances.

According to Proverbs 4:23, Solomon urges us to guard our hearts with all diligence, for out of them is the wellspring of life. What bubbles up on our faces and into our actions is a direct reflection of the state of our hearts.

Earlier in the book, we talked about the story of the woman of the well in the Gospels. Jesus approaches a well in Samaria in the heat of the day and asks the woman there for a drink of water. After a series of questions between them, Jesus responds,

> Whoever drinks of the water that I will give him will never
> be thirsty again. The water that I will give him will become
> in him a spring of water welling up to eternal life." (John 4:14)

The living water that Jesus is talking about here is the Holy Spirit. When we believe in Jesus as Lord over our lives, the Holy Spirit comes and takes up residence inside our hearts. Jesus describes the Spirit here as becoming in us a spring of water welling up to eternal life. He claims that all who drink from this water will never be thirsty again. We can find true and complete satisfaction in knowing that we will get to spend eternity with our Savior.

As followers of Jesus, we should not feel forced to fake or pretend to have joy. Cheerfulness is a discipline. When cheerfulness is not what wells up out of our hearts, onto our faces, and into our actions, we should stop and reflect. We can choose to examine our hearts and actively reconnect our hearts to the wellspring of life—the person of Jesus who is available to us through the Holy Spirit. When we do this, our cheerfulness and joy can be genuine despite our circumstances. Sometimes, we need a heart check.

HEART CHECK

My husband is a cardiologist and spends much of his time examining people's hearts. There are a couple of things he does to check someone's heart:

1. He uses a stethoscope to listen to their heartbeat. Usually, a nurse checks a person's pulse or heart rate.
2. He asks the person good questions to gain an accurate diagnosis.
3. He might order an ultrasound or an echocardiogram, maybe an EKG, or other tests to get a better picture of what is going on inside the heart.
4. He might send someone home with a heart monitor to wear for several days or a couple of weeks.

The severity of what he is hearing or seeing will determine what tests he orders and what the next steps are. Other times, a patient comes in having a heart attack, and that requires immediate action from the medical team.

When we talk about the "heart" in spiritual circles, we talk about the seat of our emotions and connections, not usually the physical heart inside your body. So when I say "heart check," I am talking more about a check on our souls and our minds. The Bible talks about the heart this way, so we will use the same train of thought. Jesus was a great listener, and He asked a lot of questions. He asked questions that cut straight to the heart of the matter. He met a religious leader named Nicodemus, who had come to see Him under the cover of the night so he wouldn't be seen. Jesus explained the gospel to him. In John 3, Nicodemus said to Him, "How can these things be?" Jesus answered him,

> "Are you the teacher of Israel and yet you do not understand these things? Truly, truly, I say to you, we speak of what we know, and bear witness to what we have seen, but you do not receive our testimony. If I have told you earthly things and you do not believe, how can you believe if I tell you heavenly things?" (John 3:10–12)

Jesus asks him questions in response to his questions. This was often how Jesus taught. He asked questions that stopped people in their tracks. He asked questions that would give people a reason to pause and think— a reason to examine their hearts.

Remember the woman at the well in John 4? He told her, "Go, call your husband, and come here," and she said, "I have no husband." Jesus replied, "You are right in saying, 'I have no husband'; for you have had five husbands, and the one you now have is not your husband" (John 4:16–18). Jesus had a way of getting straight to the point. He peeled back the layers and exposed the things that mattered most, often hidden. Their conversation revealed what was going on in her heart. This is how He examined hearts while He was on earth. Now, the Holy Spirit acts as the heart examiner.

God can see our hearts. Even more precise than an echocardiogram or an ultrasound, God can look underneath all the layers and straight to our soul. This truth is apparent throughout the Bible, from the Old Testament to the New Testament. When choosing which of Jesse's sons would become the king, he chose David, the most unlikely candidate. The young boy who was out tending the sheep, the one who looked least like a king. Samuel records, "Man looks on the outward appearance, but the Lord looks on the heart." (1 Sam. 16:7). God didn't care about David's stature or outward appearance, or maybe He did. Maybe He picked the most unlikely candidate so people would truly see His power on display throughout the young boy's life. Scripture records that David grew to be "a man after [God's] own heart" (1 Sam. 13:14). David understood that God saw his heart. It is apparent in his writings in Psalms. The psalms of David are full of heartfelt petitions to God. After David had committed terrible sins—adultery, murder, lying, he penned this psalm:

> All my longings lie open before you, Lord;
> my sighing is not hidden from you.
> My heart pounds, my strength fails me;
> even the light has gone from my eyes. (Ps. 38:9–10, NIV)

David understood on a deep level that God saw straight into his heart. Even in his sin, he didn't hide from God. He knew he couldn't. The fact that God could see his heart didn't scare David; it comforted him. He appealed to God, talked to God, sang to God, and didn't hide from God. David's reactions are such a good example to us.

When Jesus came on the scene, He further proved this point. In Luke 5:22, we see a conversation between Jesus and His disciples. It got quiet around the circle, "When Jesus perceived their thoughts, He answered them, "Why do you question in your hearts?" Jesus reveals that the heart isn't a secret part to Him yet again. How crazy this must have been for the disciples. They were sitting around the circle thinking inside their own heads only to have Jesus speak their very secret thoughts out loud to them.

To check our hearts, we can ask ourselves a couple of questions.

- What are my secret thoughts?
- How am I spending my time?
- Where am I putting my focus?
- Have I prayed today?
- How am I treating those I love? Strangers?

Like David, may we not be afraid of having our hearts examined. Some people have medical anxiety and are afraid to go to the doctor. If we don't go for regular checkups, we may end up in an emergency situation. If we go for regular checkups, we can often avoid a significant event like a heart attack through preventative measures and medications. The same is true for our spiritual hearts. Let's do regular checks so we don't end up in an urgent situation. When we exercise our spiritual muscles and disciplines regularly, we stay in touch with God and His plan for our lives.

ETERNITY IN MIND

As our little girl began to sit and watch a princess movie or character TV show, she began asking questions. When a sad part would come in the movie, she would repeatedly ask me, "Are they happy, Mama?" She was so bothered when a character was sad or when something happened to them that she wouldn't settle until it was resolved. Innately, she knew that something was wrong, and she had a strong desire to see it made right.

Whether it was Cinderella's stepsisters treating her unkindly or Mickey Mouse trying to solve a problem, she always asked, "Are they happy, Mommy?" I repeatedly reassured her, "Yes, baby, I think they are happy now." She wanted my reassurance that everything would turn out okay and that the characters she loved would be happy and cheerful. She needed me to remind her that the present danger faced by the characters had been avoided. I didn't teach her to worry about that; it was just her instinct.

We all share a little bit of that same desire. We want things to turn out well. We all want a happy ending. The thing about us as followers of Jesus is that we are promised and assured of the ultimate happy ending, but so often, we live as if we don't believe that is true.

As we wrap up our study together, I want to challenge you in your cheerfulness. To choose cheer, we can put our problems into perspective by keeping eternity in mind. When we chase joy and cheer in things outside of Jesus, we are working for the things that are seen and wasting away. Colossians 3:2 (NIV) reminds us, "Set your minds on things above, not on earthly things." And Jesus Himself says,

> I am the vine; you are the branches. Whoever abides in me and I in him, he it is that bears much fruit, for apart from me you can do nothing." (John 15:5)

When we abide in God's presence, we will choose cheer that comes up from a wellspring of eternal life and will last forever.

I am convinced that our joy and our cheerfulness are rooted in our understanding of eternity. When we have an eternal perspective, we know what we face here on earth is temporary. We often have a limited view of our eternal home. Heaven will be so much more than gold streets and pearly gates. Earthly riches will fade in the presence of our infinite God. Gold will lose its shine in the brilliant light of God's presence. Gold, one of our most precious materials on earth, will be the ground we walk on in our eternal home. Everything valuable here will fade in the light of our Risen King in His heavenly dwelling.

Erin is one of my dear friends with whom I served in ministry. We look nothing alike. Where I am short and have straight, dark hair; she is tall and slim, has the brightest smile, and has beautiful red ringlets. Our friendship developed quickly as we worked together day in and day out over the years. Once our jobs changed, although we didn't see each other every day, we stayed in touch. When we did get together, we would pick up like we never left off.

I got a call from Erin one day that I'll never forget. My precious friend had received the worst news. She had cancer, a lot of it, and would need surgery and treatment quickly. We immediately began praying, begging God for her healing. I checked on Erin regularly throughout her journey and as she started her treatment, she let me know that the doctors predicted she would lose all of her hair from her chemo regimen.

For anyone, this is a hard reality to swallow. For a female, our hair is such an essential part of who we are, and our outward appearance. But for my friend, Erin, it was even more devastating. She might not say this, but her hair was her crowning glory. It was so beautiful and unique. The gorgeous red color and beautiful curls were an example of God's handiwork. Tears fell from my eyes as she told me her plans to shave her head once her hair started to fall out. She felt that would be easier and less traumatic than having chunks falling out every day for weeks. I offered to go with her to the salon when she had this done.

As I prayed for her leading up to this day, I was reminded that she would have hair again in heaven, but I still mourned for this earthly loss. Our friend Kayla joined us as we began the day in the salon. Erin wanted to go first thing and get it over with, out of the way. As we looked in the mirror and held hands, our faces didn't look cheerful, but joy was still present in our spirits. It may have been an incredibly hard moment, but we were together.

Our friend was receiving treatment, and the prognosis looked hopeful. I felt that my friend would be okay, and that God would carry her through this incredibly challenging season. At Erin's request, we turned this awful day into a day of beauty. I did her makeup, and we picked out some scarves to cover her now bald head. It ended up being a really beautiful day.

I had coffee with Erin just the other day, and she is doing remarkably well. Her scans are coming back clear, and her hair is growing back in little sprigs, curls starting to show. I am so grateful for her recovery and healing. Seeing her will always remind me of the fragility of life and to be grateful for each day.

Erin works as a hospital chaplain. I am amazed at how God uses her experience to minister to others. As we sipped our coffee, she shared a story with me of one of her recent patients whom she had walked with from diagnosis to death. Erin described the questions and struggles the man discussed when faced with the likelihood of an imminent death and how those fears turned into peace as time went on. As she described his last days, she commented on the beauty of watching heaven dip down to earth. Leading up to his death, sleep overtook most of his days, but one morning, as my friend entered his room, she said he was looking up and smiling, his face radiant. She was taken aback and had never seen such pure joy and peace. She asked him, "Do you see Jesus?" He lowered his eyes, smiled at her, and looked back up. Chills ran down my arms as she described this moment.

Our eternal promise is so much more than pearl gates and gold streets. Our eternal promise is that we get to be with God forever. We get to live and stay in His presence without any of the hurt and distractions of this world. In Revelation, John writes:

> He will wipe away every tear from their eyes, and death shall be no more, neither shall there be mourning, nor crying, nor pain anymore, for the former things have passed away. (Rev. 21:4)

We have an eternity to look forward to, something to celebrate. How it is now is not how it will always be. This promise alone should give us reason to be cheerful every day we are here on earth.

In John 16:33, Jesus promises His disciples and us today that we will face trouble on this side of eternity. He also promises that He will be with us and that we can experience His cheer and joy because He has overcome the world. One of my former pastors used to say, "I cheated. I read the back of the book, and I know who wins." We can access supernatural joy when we believe that Jesus has overcome the world and that we are just living in the in-between. We can live in a victorious mindset instead of a victim mindset. We can choose to be close to Jesus and be cheerful despite our circumstances.

We know that cheerfulness is a choice, we see what cheats us from cheerfulness, we've discussed practical plans for growing closer to Jesus and experiencing more of his joy in our lives. The message is simple: Choose Cheer.

When you're happy, choose cheer.

When you're sad, choose cheer.

When things are going great, choose cheer.

And when things aren't, choose cheer.

If you're single, choose cheer.

If you're in a relationship, choose cheer.

When you feel in control, choose cheer.

When you feel out of control, choose cheer.

In interactions with your family, choose cheer.

In interactions with strangers, choose cheer.

In the small things, choose cheer.

In the big things, choose cheer.

It's a choice.

It's a continual choice again and again, and every time I choose cheer, I choose Jesus.

 Cheer Practice

5—Breath Prayers

Pray this scripture on an inhale and exhale.

- Inhale: one, two, three, four
- Exhale: five, six, seven, eight
- Try breathing and meditating on the words or saying the words aloud on those counts.
- Inhale: God has set eternity
- Exhale: in our hearts
  (Eccles. 3:11)

- Inhale: Be of good cheer
- Exhale: I have overcome the world
  (John 16:33)

6—Scripture Callout

Let's memorize this scripture together.
Our ninth callout:

> "Choose this day whom you will serve, whether the gods your fathers served in the region beyond the River, or the gods of the Amorites in whose land you dwell. But as for me and my house, we will serve the LORD." (Josh. 24:15)

Practice saying this verse out loud, repeat it, write it down, and put it somewhere that you can see it.

7—Gratitude Challenge

I believe that gratitude is the best prescription for cheerfulness. When we think about the things we are grateful for, it is hard to stay focused on our challenging circumstances. Thankfulness is not always something that comes natural to us. We have to practice.

I encourage you to write down three things that you are grateful for today. This could be in relation to what we've studied in this chapter or just related to something in your life right now. I encourage you to think of something different from the last chapter.

Thank you, Jesus, for:

_____

_____

_____

8—Spread Some Cheer

TODAY'S CHEER CHALLENGE: HOW CAN YOU INTENTIONALLY SPREAD CHEER TODAY?

In this chapter, we discussed how Choosing Cheer requires our intentionality. It is a choice. How can you intentionally spread cheer today? Intention can begin with pausing. When we pause, we make room for the Holy Spirit to lead our next step. One example that comes to mind is a member of the Life Group I lead at our church on Sunday mornings was preparing for a big test. One of the other members in our group took out their phone and made a calendar reminder for the day of his test to prompt them to pray on that day. This simple step moved a simple, "I'll pray for you" to the next level. When we are intentional with our time and our choices, it increases our own joy and the joy of those around us.

TEN

The Cheerfulness Challenge

We have learned together that cheerfulness is a command and a promise from Jesus. While yes He promises us that we will have trouble, He also promises us that we can have cheer despite our circumstances. The Bible talks about the source of our joy, the Holy Spirit. Joy is best experienced when we practice contentment, surrender, prayer, and intentionality. It is important for us to understand this concept not only from a purely biblical perspective but also from the perspective of human experience.

Many studies have proven a direct correlation between a person's religious involvement and happiness. As someone who has studied social sciences, I love when science backs up what the Bible has said for centuries. *Time* magazine released an interesting article that looked at many studies published on the connection between religion and happiness. Despite differing opinions and faiths, the overwhelming conclusion of the studies is that there is an absolute connection between religion and happiness (Walsh

2017). In a more recent article by Pew Research Group, their analysis found that in the United States and other countries, "regular participation in a religious community is linked with higher levels of happiness and civic engagement" (Mitchell 2019).

Research not only shows that religious participants are happier than those who do not participate in religion, but many studies show that the happiness and belonging experienced from a religious practice can increase life expectancy. According to Dan Buettner and National Geographic's research on Blue Zones, a longevity study of areas of the world where people live the longest, one of the key factors of living longer is belonging to a faith-based community. Their research shows "that attending faith-based services four times per month will add 4-14 years of life expectancy" (Buettner and Skemp 2016). This suggestion starkly contrasts the US Surgeon General's report we discussed in chapter 2, where loneliness can increase premature death (Office of the Surgeon General (OSG) 2023). Proverbs 17:22 (NIV) echoes this when it says, "A cheerful heart is good medicine, but a crushed spirit dries up the bones."

These studies identify happiness, but we, as followers of Jesus, know that what they are describing is deeper than happiness—it is true joy. We know that we are made in the image of a communal God, and we understand that God placed the desire for belonging and connection in humanity in us. Living a life of connection to God and connection to those around us allows us to experience His joy.

A LIFE MARKED WITH JOY

When considering a life lived with joy, a very special person comes to mind. Sharline had a laugh that would precede her, along with her jingling bracelets and earrings. Some of my earliest childhood memories include her entering the house laden with gifts for every holiday and special occasion. She was always there, and for a long time, I thought we were biologically related. Sharline was a teacher, and her classroom was a few doors down from my dad's. When my dad was a young and inexperienced teacher, she took him under her wing and adopted us as her family. Shortly after, when I was four years old, and my grandmother was dying, I was hospitalized for a virus in a different hospital. Sharline stayed with me to allow my parents to go back and forth to spend the last hours with my grandmother. My parents remark that at that time, they knew Sharline was more than a good friend; she was family. She was present at every ball game, performance, pageant, graduation.

Sharline never married and never had kids of her own, but she was deeply connected. She loved with her whole self. When she died, I was struck by the image of Jesus's love, which I witnessed through her love for me. She had no reason to love me and invest in me. We weren't connected by blood, we lived two hours apart, she was retired and no longer teaching down the hall from my dad, but she kept on showing up and kept on loving us. It is one of the most tangible expressions I have received that has helped me understand God's love for me. It is unearned, undeserved,

but given without restraint. I long to pick up the phone and
FaceTime her and hear her laugh echo through my speakers. I
envisioned her sitting at my daughter's birthday party, knowing
she would have made the trip and been there with a smile and a
gift. When I think of her, I ask God to give me the joy that she
had. The type of joy that is contagious and is lived out in action.
I want my life to be marked by the joy of Jesus, and after reading
this book, I hope your desire is the same.

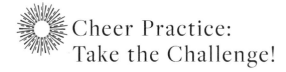

Cheer Practice: Take the Challenge!

This is the final Cheer Practice before the big game or
competition. We've come a long way together on our journey toward Choosing Cheer. I pray this is only the beginning of a life soaked in the fullness of the joy of Jesus. John
16:24 in the Message translation says, "Your joy will be a
river overflowing its banks!" My prayer for you is to experience this joy, overflowing into all areas of your life.

This book means nothing if we don't put it into practice. Take this challenge, this manifesto, if you will, and
read it daily. Print it, write it, and put it somewhere where
you can read it daily. I challenge you to read it every day for
thirty days and at the end of the thirty-day period, see if
you are experiencing more of the joy of Jesus.

The Cheerfulness Challenge

I commit to pursue the joy of Jesus regardless of my circumstance.

I recognize that my closeness with Christ has a direct correlation to my cheerfulness.

The attitude of my heart will show up on my face and spill into my actions with others.

I confess that I cannot do this on my own and I need the help of the Holy Spirit. I Choose Cheer today.

Acknowledgments

A finished book is the culmination of collective support. I am grateful beyond measure for those who supported me in this process.

I am blessed with the best family support system. Thank you to Preston, my husband, my best friend, and my biggest cheerleader. You are the light that brings cheer to all of my days. Thank you for dreaming and brainstorming with me, editing and providing feedback. To be a doctor, you are surprisingly great at grammar and creative writing. Thank you for creating space for me to write, even amidst our crazy schedules. I simply could not have done this without you.

My parents ignited my love for books as they spent countless hours reading to me as a young girl. Thank you seems inadequate. Mom, you instilled the values of cheerfulness in me from the time I could hold pom-poms. I am so grateful for your constant encouragement and hours on the phone of me asking you, "What do you think about this?" No one has listened to more sermons, lessons, or read more of my content than you. Daddy, thank you for always supporting me with your quiet strength and countless hours of entertaining Josie Lou. Thank you for always being my listening ear and my encouraging word when I feel overwhelmed or want to give up.

Thank you to my fabulous in-laws. To Bella, thank you for always believing and supporting my dream. Thank you for donating a computer, allowing me to use your office, and for babysitting Josie Lou so I could have quiet time to write. To RB, thank you for your belief in God's gifts in my life. Thank you for supporting the Choosing Cheer ministry—it means more to me than you will ever know. Thank you both for raising a man of God that I get to love and call my own. It takes a village, and I am so glad you are in mine.

I was blessed by a lovely group of friends and prayer warriors who served as first readers on this project. Susan, Kim, Aunt Cheryl, Mrs. Ann, Brandon, Sissy, Michelle, Mrs. Beth, Lauren, Bethany and Mrs. Patty, thank you for making this book better.

Thank you to Chip MacGregor, my coworker, literary agent, and friend, for believing in me and asking me to write this book proposal. Thank you for seeing something in me that I didn't see in myself and supporting me every step of the way.

Thank you to Fiona and the wonderful team at Morehouse. Thank you for believing in me and being so kind and easy to work with. You have made publishing my first book a delightful experience.

Above all, thank you to Jesus for speaking to me and speaking through me. My prayer is that every word on these pages would point you closer to Him and help you to experience more of His joy in your life.

Cheers!

Nicolet

Group Study Questions

CHAPTER 1—CHOICES

- Do you enjoy making decisions/choices or fear them?
- In what type of situation have you had to choose joy over sorrow? How did that impact you and your walk with Jesus or those around you?
- Consider the lesson on the Other Boats. When have you gone through a trial and realized its impact on those around you? Have you been an "other boat" for someone else?

CHAPTER 2—PROMISES

- Think about a time when you were lost or alone. How did you feel in those moments? Have you ever felt emotionally or spiritually alone? What made you feel secure again?
- Like my brother had confidence in my dad's ability to find him, how can you cultivate a similar trust in Jesus

during challenging times? What practices can help strengthen that trust?

- Reflect on the concept of "fullness of joy." What does it mean to you to experience joy in its fullness, rather than just in moments? How can you seek out and cultivate joy in your life?

- What is your favorite gift you've ever received?

3—CHALLENGES

- Reflect on a challenge you are currently facing. How can you Choose Cheer without ignoring the problems/hardships around you?

- When considering Jesus's suffering on the cross, what are your thoughts about his inner joy? Is this a new thought or have you considered this before?

- What challenges have you faced, or are you facing, that challenge your cheerfulness?

- Reflect on James's statement to "consider it pure joy . . . whenever you face trials of many kinds" (James 1:2). This is a hard statement for us to swallow. What does this verse mean to you?

CHAPTER 4—CONFUSED CONNECTIONS

- Do you have a memory box? What's the most important thing to you in it?

- Do you know someone who lives a solitary life? How can you encourage them or reach out to them?
- What steps can you take to foster deeper connections?
- What ideas do you have in your head about what a romantic relationship should look like? How do you think God's ideas about romance differ from the concept given to us by the world, not only sexually but emotionally as well?
- Jesus displayed incredible forgiveness to His closest friends, the disciples. Are there areas of your life where you are harboring unforgiveness?

CHAPTER 5—COMPARISON

- What runs through your mind when you are "not" thinking?
- Who are you trying to please?
- In what areas of your life do you need to sound the "Fake Life!" alarm?
- How does comparison relate to our cheerfulness/joy?

CHAPTER 6—CONTROL

- Like Josie and her bubbles, what are you straining your neck behind or forwards to see?
- In doing so, what could you be missing in the present?

- What area of your life do you need to release control to Jesus? What practical steps can you take toward that?

CHAPTER 7—HELPER

- If you are honest, what areas of life do you need some help?
- How do we set our minds on things of the Spirit as talked about in Romans 8?
- What ideas/thoughts do you have about the Holy Spirit and His role in your life?
- How does the promise of the Holy Spirit being with you change your perspective on facing difficulties? In what specific situations can you remind yourself that you are not alone?

CHAPTER 8—PRAYER

- Jesus modeled for us what it looked like to pray for others. Who are you feeling led to pray for?
- Jesus prayed for us to have unity as His followers. Where do you see unity in the church? Where is it lacking?
- How is our prayer life connected to our joy/cheer?

CHAPTER 9—CHEERFUL

- Do you ever "try on" cheer (or joy) and take it off?

- In what ways can you intentionally keep eternity in mind?
- What's one way you can choose cheer today?

CHAPTER 10—THE CHEERFULNESS CHALLENGE

- Considering this challenge, what stands out the most to you?
- What has been the most challenging part of Choosing Cheer?
- What is your biggest takeaway from this study?

Bibliography

Baker, Warren. 2013. *Hebrew-Greek Key Word Study Bible: Key Insights into God's Word : ESV, English Standard Version*. New version. Chattanooga, TN: AMG Publishers.

Barclay, William, ed. 2017. *The Gospel of John*. The New Daily Study Bible. Louisville, KY: Westminster John Knox Press.

Buettner, Dan, and Sam Skemp. 2016. "Blue Zones: Lessons from the World's Longest Lived." *American Journal of Lifestyle Medicine* 10 (5): 318–21. https://doi.org/10.1177/1559827616637066.

Garrison, Charles E. 2021. *A Trilogy of Poetry for the Future*. Grace Impact Publishing.

Mitchell, Travis. 2019. "Religion's Relationship to Happiness, Civic Engagement and Health Around the World." *Pew Research Center* (blog). January 31, 2019. https://www.pewresearch.org/religion/2019/01/31/religions-relationship-to-happiness-civic-engagement-and-health-around-the-world/.

Office of the Surgeon General (OSG). 2023. *Our Epidemic of Loneliness and Isolation: The U.S. Surgeon General's Advisory on the Healing Effects of Social Connection and Community*. Publications and Reports of the Surgeon General. Washington (DC): US Department of Health and Human Services. http://www.ncbi.nlm.nih.gov/books/NBK595227/.

Walsh, Bryan. 2017. "Does Spirituality Make You Happy?" *Time*. August 7, 2017. https://time.com/4856978/spirituality-religion-happiness/.

References

Ayars, Matthew I. 2023. *The Holy Spirit: An Introduction*. Franklin, Tennessee: Seedbed Publishing.

Baker, Warren. 2013. *Hebrew-Greek Key Word Study Bible: Key Insights into God's Word : ESV, English Standard Version*. New version. AMG Publishers.

Barclay, William, ed. 2017. *The Gospel of John*. The New Daily Study Bible. Westminster John Knox Press.

Buettner, Dan, and Sam Skemp. 2016. "Blue Zones: Lessons From the World's Longest Lived." *American Journal of Lifestyle Medicine* 10 (5): 318–21. https://doi.org/10.1177/1559827616637066.

Garrison, Charles E. 2021. *A Trilogy of Poetry for the Future*. Grace Impact Publishing.

Lewis, C. S. 2005. *The Chronicles of Narnia. Book 7: The Last Battle*. New York: HarperTrophy.

Mitchell, Travis. 2019. "Religion's Relationship to Happiness, Civic Engagement and Health Around the World." *Pew Research Center* (blog). January 31, 2019. https://www.pewresearch.org/religion/2019/01/31/religions-relationship-to-happiness-civic-engagement-and-health-around-the-world/.

Office of the Surgeon General (OSG). 2023. *Our Epidemic of Loneliness and Isolation: The U.S. Surgeon General's Advisory on the*

Healing Effects of Social Connection and Community. Publications and Reports of the Surgeon General. US Department of Health and Human Services. http://www.ncbi.nlm.nih.gov /books/NBK595227/.

Roosevelt, Theodore. 1905. "Comparison Is the Thief of Joy."

Walsh, Bryan. 2017. "Does Spirituality Make You Happy?" *Time.* August 7, 2017. https://time.com/4856978/spirituality -religion-happiness/.